SPACE MISTAKES

Timothy Knapman

Illustrated by Seb Burnett

Chapter 1
Oops!

Oliver Jolly was the kindest, friendliest and most genial young man who had ever enrolled on the Peace Management programme at the Intergalactic Space Academy. So it came as a huge surprise to him – and to everyone else – when he brought the universe to the very brink of all-out war one Thursday afternoon.

And all because of a blueberry muffin.

This was big news. There hadn't been a war anywhere in the universe for thirty years. After billions of centuries spent fighting one another for no good reason, the countless different peoples of the countless different planets had suddenly realized – much to their own surprise – that they'd had enough. Instead of settling their arguments by laying waste to one another's homes, from now on they were just going to pop round for a cup of tea and a chat.

No one was quite sure why.

Of course, wars are:

a) expensive

b) noisy and, most of all,

c) incredibly stupid.

But that had never stopped anyone fighting them in the past. On the contrary, the sheer pointless awfulness of the whole thing seemed to be the reason they all kept doing it. And then, without any warning, everybody woke up one morning and just thought *Nah.* They hung up their laser blasters, unplugged their plasma cannons and decided that their terrifying battle stations should be painted pale green and turned into coffee bars.

It was all very mysterious.

For years, historians tried to explain why this extraordinary and entirely unprecedented thing had happened. They eventually agreed that 'profound socio-economic undercurrents promoted pacifistic trends in the galactic population that finally reached critical mass'.

Which is what historians always say when what they *really* mean is: 'Search me.'

Besides, it didn't really matter *why* everyone had stopped fighting because it turned out they all found peace to be rather agreeable. In fact, the only really contentious question was why they hadn't tried it earlier.

And the very best thing about peace?

It was the food, obviously.

Instead of having to hide, shivering, in the flaming ruins of their intergalactic spaceships eating whatever revolting scraps they could find in the vending machines, everyone could now travel across the universe on holiday and feast on all kinds of delicious dishes. There were crab cakes from the Crab Nebula and Alpha Centauri spaghetti; there were subatomic sandwiches and dark matter chocolate; there were Big Bang bean burgers and pulsar pizzas – delicious!

Many enjoyed the food on other planets so much that they decided to move there permanently, and soon enough the universe was a glorious mixture of different kinds of peoples – humanoids, yes, but also plenty of bright blue shrews and superintelligent millipedes, walking fish folk and giant space grasshoppers – all living (and eating) together in harmony.

Until, that is, an otherwise normal Thursday afternoon and Oliver's blueberry muffin.

***

Thursday itself had started promisingly. It was the day Oliver Jolly and the rest of his classmates graduated from the Intergalactic Space Academy. The students wore their smartest uniforms and gathered in the Palace of Universal Peace – the most majestic building on the Galactic Capital Planet (which had once been called 'Earth'). The palace was constructed almost entirely of golden glass, so that when you entered it, it felt like you were walking into a starbeam.

As part of the ceremony, there was a speech from His Coolness, King Serenity the Untroubled, probably the wisest – and certainly the most relaxed – being in the universe. He lolled comfortably in his hammock throne, and gave the students plenty of useful advice about how they could live long, happy and fulfilling lives, before he dozed back off to sleep again. There was (quiet) applause – they didn't want to wake King Serenity – as the certificates were handed out. Prizes were awarded (Oliver won Kindest Student, Friendliest Student *and* Most Genial Student – which was a record). Proud parents took countless pictures and videos and soon everyone decided they felt a bit peckish and it was time to head off to the party afterwards.

'What a lovely spread!' said the students' mums as they surveyed the huge and tempting banquet laid out before them.

'Nom nom nom,' said the students' dads, who had already started stuffing themselves.

Oliver looked around the room for his own father. Alastair Jolly was a distinguished official in the Ministry of Universal Harmony and he beamed proudly at his son.

'Well done,' he said, shaking Oliver's hand. 'Sorry I couldn't be at the ceremony but I was too busy welcoming all our visitors.' As well as the students and their relatives, the room was bursting with important guests from all the major civilizations in the universe.

'Look at them all,' Oliver's dad went on. 'Everyone's chatting away happily to one another. It's hard to believe that just thirty short years ago, they were all at one another's throats.'

'I always think it's better to look forward rather than back,' said Oliver.

'Quite right,' said his dad. 'The past is gone. The future is bright. Talking of a bright future, have you decided what you want to do with your life yet?'

'I just want to be useful,' said Oliver. 'I was hoping to get a job polishing asteroids or refurbishing moons, perhaps, at one of the intergalactic agencies.'

'I think a record-breaking triple prize-winner can afford to set his sights a little higher,' said his dad kindly. 'What do you think about spending your life strengthening the ties of peace between creatures across the universe?'

'Do you mean a job at the Ministry, with you?' gasped Oliver. 'That would be a dream come true! But I haven't had any practical experience yet. Everything I've learned has been in the classroom.'

'I think they should have given you the prize for Most Modest Student too,' chuckled his dad. 'You're just the sort of young person we're looking for. You start on Monday.'

Oliver was so thrilled that he was rendered speechless and he just goggled at his dad for a moment. At last he managed to splutter, 'That is wonderful! Thank you so much!'

'There's no need to thank me,' his dad shrugged. 'Someone as talented as you deserves nothing less. Congratulations: a long and comfortable future awaits you. In fact, I see my colleagues from the Ministry have just come in. Shall we go over and meet them?'

'I'd love to,' said Oliver, 'but I'd just like to thank King Serenity for his speech first.' Oliver's professors were always telling him how important it was to say 'please' and 'thank you'. He knew they'd be proud of him.

King Serenity was fast asleep, his large, scaly purple stomach rising and falling in time to the gentle sound of his snoring.

Oliver coughed quietly and whispered, 'Your Coolness?'

The King's kindly green eyes opened. He looked Oliver up and down and uttered the traditional greeting of his people: ''Sup, dude? I was having a snooze.'

Oliver gave the traditional response: 'Stuff, geezer.'

The King smiled. 'Stuff? What kind?' he asked.

'I just wanted to say thank you for your wonderful speech,' said Oliver.

'No sweat,' replied the King and he rolled over to go back to sleep.

'Er, sorry, Your Coolness,' Oliver continued, 'I just wanted to give you this gift, as a token of our gratitude.' He reached into his pocket and brought out a little box.

Oliver had read that the King loved cakes, especially cakes with fruit in them. He wanted to show the King how grateful he and his classmates were for his wonderful speech, so he had decided to do something very special. Rather than just *buying* a fruit cake from any corner fruit cake store and giving it to the King, he had decided to *bake* him one – and not just any fruit cake, but something the King would never forget. So Oliver had gone to the library and consulted the most ancient texts that dated right back to when this planet had still been called 'Earth'. There he read about wild and wonderful fruit cakes and puddings that hadn't been baked for so many centuries they had now become the stuff of legend: Dundee cakes, scones, bread and butter pudding, spotted dick ... They all sounded very exotic and strange!

At last he had found a cookery book that had been wrapped in heavy chains and shoved right to the back of the shelf. The chains were so old and rusted and brittle that he could snap them apart easily. He'd opened the book, coughed a lot because it was covered in dust, and started to read.

That was where he discovered it, the perfect little cake with fruit in it: the blueberry muffin. As far as he could see, no one had baked a blueberry muffin in over five hundred years. The King would be the first creature in all that time to taste one – he was bound to love it and he'd realize how much effort Oliver had gone to and he'd be delighted.

What could possibly go wrong?

Just the thought of making the King happy made Oliver glow. He watched carefully as the King opened the box and brought out the little cake. The King licked his lips as he turned the muffin around in his long, scaly purple fingers.

'Looks scrummy,' he murmured, and then he took a bite. 'Ooh!' he went on. 'Yes indeed! This is the stuff!' and he popped the rest of the muffin into his mouth and chewed. 'Mmm ... Mmm ... Oh yeah. Whassiss coll, man?' he said through a wodge of crumbs.

'What's it called?' Oliver said. 'It's a little delicacy that hasn't been baked in five hundred years. It's a blueberry muffin.'

The King stopped chewing at once.

'Whaddid yoosay?'

'What did I say?' Oliver said. Come to think of it, it was rather a silly name, so Oliver smiled even more broadly as he said very clearly, to avoid any further confusion, 'It's ... a ... blueberry ... muffin.'

Oliver wasn't entirely sure what would happen next. Maybe the King would smile, swallow, say thank you and go back to sleep. Maybe he would enfold him in a huge bear hug and ask him for the recipe. Maybe he would invite him to marry one of his daughters.

As it turned out, the King did none of these things. Interestingly, he did the one thing Oliver *didn't* expect, which was this: he roared the words 'BLUEBERRY MUFFIN?' in a very loud and angry voice, and spat what was left of the blueberry muffin straight back in Oliver's face. Then His Coolness, King Serenity the Untroubled, probably the wisest – and certainly the most relaxed – being in the universe, sprang out of his hammock throne, grabbed Oliver by the throat and the pair of them went crashing into the buffet table, sending food flying everywhere.

A lump of extremely runny Milky Whey cheese turned somersaults in the air before landing – with a very rude noise – all over the principal of the Intergalactic Space Academy, ruining both her afternoon *and* her very expensive dress in a single splat. The Twanganese prime minister found this hilarious, pointed at her and laughed. The principal of the Intergalactic Space Academy was a proud person who'd spent a fortune on her dress, so she picked up a fistful of parsec pie and threw it at the Twanganese prime minister to shut him up. The fistful of pie missed the Twanganese prime minister and hit the Voravian envoy instead. The Voravian envoy's bodyguards started pelting the principal of the Intergalactic Space Academy with Ice Giant ice cream.

The principal ducked, and the ice cream landed in a huge puddle that the Omplooviate ambassador slipped in, sending him skidding across the floor, knocking over the distinguished guests from all the major civilizations in the universe as he went. He reached out wildly for something to hold on to. Unfortunately, the only thing he managed to grab was the top of the Sebnethian ambassador's trousers, which he ripped off before landing head first in the subatomic sandwiches.

There is no greater insult in Sebnethian culture than exposing someone's flowery underwear in a public place, so the Sebnethian ambassador went squawking

after the Omplooviate ambassador, and tried to pull his nose off.

There is no greater insult in Omplooviate culture than pulling someone's nose off, so the Omplooviate ambassador immediately declared war on the Sebnethian Empire.

Thankfully, as the Sebnethian ambassador was still trying to pull his nose off, all the Omplooviate ambassador could say was 'I decware law ob dee Sebbeffian Embire!' so it didn't count.

Not that anyone was listening anyway, because by now all the distinguished guests from all the major civilizations in the universe were completely covered in cream and custard and were declaring war on one another left, right and centre.

Oliver's dad and his colleagues from the Ministry of Universal Harmony went rushing around trying to restore universal harmony. It wasn't easy.

'What in all the glittering galaxy is going on, Oliver?' asked his dad. 'We finally managed to achieve universal harmony after billions of centuries of war, and you've very nearly ruined it in less than twenty minutes!'

All Oliver could say in reply was 'Urg!' because King Serenity the Untroubled, probably the wisest – and certainly the most relaxed – being in the universe, was still attempting to throttle him. With a tremendous effort, Oliver's father managed to drag the King off and sat him in a darkened room to calm down.

'I promise you, I have no idea why the King got so angry,' Oliver sputtered hoarsely when his dad came back. 'All I said was "It's a blueberry muffin" and he went berserk!'

'Well, why in jumping Jupiter did you say that?' asked his dad.

'Because I'd just given him a blueberry muffin and he'd asked me what it was,' said Oliver. 'I thought he'd be flattered. They're delicious and nobody's baked any in five hundred years.'

'Well of course nobody's baked any in five hundred years!' cried his dad. 'That's because the words "blueberry muffin" sound exactly like the worst possible insult in King Serenity's home language.'

'Ah,' said Oliver.

'The last time someone tried to give one of King Serenity's ancestors a blueberry muffin, it started a war that lasted for a thousand years!' said his dad.

'Oops!' said Oliver. 'No wonder the cookery book was wrapped in heavy chains.'

'Why don't you know that?' asked his dad. 'You're a star student!'

'I didn't take the history module,' said Oliver. 'I always think it's better to look—'

Alastair Jolly finished his son's sentence for him: ' ... forward rather than back,' and he buried his head in his hands.

Oliver looked around. The room was quieter now. His dad's colleagues from the Ministry had succeeded in calming everyone down – even if that had meant throwing buckets of cold water over them – and the distinguished guests from all the major civilizations in the universe were limping soggily out of the room and apologizing for those horrible things they'd said about each other's mums.

Oliver was a positive person, and very soon he was looking on the bright side again. 'Could have been worse,' he said. 'So Dad, what time do you want me to show up at the Ministry on Monday?'

One of his dad's colleagues overheard this and answered Oliver with a noise that was so rude, Oliver realized he was never going to be allowed anywhere near the Ministry of Universal Harmony, not even to polish asteroids.

'Ah,' he said. 'So what *am* I going to do now?'

Chapter 2

A galaxy far, far, far, far, far away

What do you do with a young man who has brought the universe to the very brink of all-out war, armed only with a blueberry muffin?

This was a difficult decision, and so it was referred to the Council of the Wise Brains. The Wise Brains were just that: the brains of the universe's wisest beings. Once their bodies had stopped working, the brains were transferred to floating globes filled with preservation fluid, where they bobbed up and down for all eternity, thinking wise thoughts and solving the problems no one else could be bothered with.

'How are you feeling this morning?' one Wise Brain would ask another at the beginning of a long day of being wise.

'Brainy, thank you very much,' the other Wise Brain would reply. 'How about you?'

'Oh brainy, certainly,' the first Wise Brain would reply. 'Very brainy.'

The Wise Brains puzzled long and hard over what to do with Oliver before determining that – for the safety of the countless different peoples of the countless different planets – he should be sent as far away as possible.

'My son has made mistakes, just like we all have,' said Alastair Jolly, who had come to plead for mercy on Oliver's behalf, 'but I know that he has it in him to be a hero. Please give him another chance.'

'Another chance is exactly what we *are* giving him,' quavered the voice of the Wisest of All Brains through the speech machine attached to her floating globe. 'Your son studied Peace Management at the academy, did he not? Well then, peace will be his mission. We will send him out into the farthest corner of the universe to make contact with planets that we have not yet reached and tell them of the joys of worlds that have turned their backs on war.'

'But we don't know what's out there,' said Oliver's dad. 'It could be extremely dangerous.'

'You show a father's concern for his son,' said another of the Wise Brains, 'but do not worry. We have sent many other SMs on such missions before.'

'What are "SMs"?' asked Oliver's dad.

'It's short for Space Mistakes,' explained the Wise Brain. 'Sorry.'

'I prefer to think of them as young men and women who have – ahem – made a bit of a mess of things and deserve another chance,' said the Wisest Brain.

'And these "SMs" all survived their missions, did they?' asked Oliver's dad.

'Of course,' said the Wisest Brain with a kind chuckle. 'Probably. They have never come back.'

'What?' said Oliver's dad.

'It is our belief that life in the farthest corner of the universe is so good, they decided to stay there,' said one of the other Brains.

'Either that or they got eaten,' said Oliver's dad.

'Ah,' said one of the other Brains. 'We had not thought of that.'

'I thought you were supposed to be wise,' said Oliver's dad.

'It is *highly unlikely* that they were eaten,' said the Wisest of All Brains.

'Yes, yes,' agreed the other Brains, 'highly unlikely.'

'That's not good enough!' said Oliver's dad. 'You can't send my son out to the farthest corner of the universe if there's even the tiniest chance he'll get eaten. I don't care what he's done.'

'Oh, all right then,' conceded the Wisest Brain grumpily. She wasn't used to people questioning her decisions. 'He's got to go but, unlike all the other Space Mistakes, he'll have a crew to go with him. That way, he's a lot less likely to get eaten. Ummm, I mean: that way he'll have a more successful mission than all the others. What do you say?'

Oliver's dad knew it was the best deal he was going to get, so he took it.

***

Of course Oliver Jolly was upset when he found out that the Wise Brains thought he was a Space Mistake – someone who was sent to the farthest corner of the universe and forgotten about – but he tried to look on the bright side. No matter what happened to him, Oliver Jolly just couldn't stop being, well, *jolly*.

'At least this way I'll have a chance to make amends,' he told his dad. 'If I push back the boundaries of the known universe and spread peace to the farthest stars, then maybe they'll see that I'm not so bad after all and invite me back.'

'But no Space Mistake has ever come back!' spluttered his dad.

'There's a first time for everything,' said Oliver.

Oliver's dad shook his head in disbelief. 'But you'll be facing terrible danger!'

'I love terrible danger!' said Oliver.

'No, you don't,' said his dad. 'You love cheese and pickle sandwiches.'

'That's right,' said Oliver. 'Silly me. I always get those two mixed up.'

'What, you always get terrible danger mixed up with cheese and pickle sandwiches?' said his dad.

'Trust me,' said Oliver. 'You don't want me packing your picnic!' and he chortled. Then he saw the worry in his dad's face and tried to reassure him. 'I'm sure I can *learn* to love terrible danger as much as cheese and pickle sandwiches. I mean, how bad can it be?'

'How bad can it be?' shrieked his dad. 'It can be terrible – and dangerous – that's how bad it can be! You could be attacked by a huge, man-eating, venom-spitting, spike-faced monster!'

'Well, you know what I always say,' said Oliver confidently. 'A huge, man-eating, venom-spitting, spike-faced monster is just a friend I haven't met yet!'

Alastair Jolly sighed and gave up. In some ways, he thought it was better that his son set off on his utterly hopeless mission with absolutely no understanding of how utterly hopeless it was. At least that way he'd have a bit of fun before he got eaten, or squished, or disintegrated on some cold and friendless planet a million billion miles away from home.

***

WANTED

BRAVE CREW FOR EXCITING NEW MISSION TO THE FARTHEST CORNER OF THE UNIVERSE

GOOD MONEY*

AMAZING BENEFITS**

ABSOLUTELY NO CHANCE OF BEING EATEN***

*Rubbish money really but as no one ever reads this bit, we can say what we like.

**No benefits at all, unless you think living in a tin can for five years is a benefit.

***Quite a big chance, actually, but what are you going to do – come back after you've been eaten and complain?

The ship that had been assigned to Oliver's mission was called the *Some Hope*. Oliver thought this was because 'some hope' was what he and his crew would be bringing to the farthest corner of the universe. In fact, it was called the *Some Hope* because when they asked the engineers who built it, 'Will this ship be able to *reach* the farthest corner of the universe?' the engineers replied, 'Some hope!'

***

The notice that went up on the board of the Skyfleet Academy wasn't the most inspiring one that had ever been posted there.

Amazingly, there were still three volunteers.

Amy Zone, who wanted to be First Mate, was the fittest person in the Academy. She ran marathons twice a day and could juggle with small cars. She was enormously enthusiastic about everything and, most of all, she loved excitement. She spent her spare time doing Extreme Sports, such as Extreme Parachute Jumping (which was like ordinary parachute jumping, except you did it in a volcano and you didn't have a parachute) and Extreme Football (which was like ordinary football, except you did it in a volcano and you didn't have a football). When asked what single thing she would change about the mission to make it more interesting, she answered, 'I wish it could be a lot more dangerous! I want to be a danger arranger – yippee!'

Stella X (she refused to give her real last name), who wanted to be Communications Officer, was an incredibly brilliant octopod who could speak seven million languages and knew rude words in five thousand more. When asked why she wanted to join this mission, she answered, 'So no one will ask me what my real last name is.' When asked 'What *is* your real last name?' she said rude words in several different languages.

Brumph, who wanted to be the ship's engineer, was a superintelligent begonia. He lived in a plant pot that had wheels on it, and this allowed him to trundle around all over the place fixing things with his twigs. He communicated by letting out funny-flavoured smells but, as Stella X could also speak the language of funny-flavoured smells (including all the rude ones), that was no barrier to him joining the crew.

***

At last, the day the mission was due to blast off had arrived. Alastair Jolly, wearing the full-dress uniform of the Ministry of Universal Harmony, tried not to cry as he prepared to wish his son farewell.

'It'll be all right, Dad,' said Oliver. 'Don't you worry.'

Oliver's dad knew perfectly well that it *wasn't* going

to be all right, but he didn't say that. He sniffed back his tears and said, 'I've got something for you.' Reaching into his pocket, he brought out a packet of cheese and pickle sandwiches in a refridgy-fresh packet. The writing on the packet said that it would keep the sandwiches 'as refridgy-squidgy as the day they were made'.

Oliver took them. 'Thanks, Dad.'

'You never know when they might come in handy,' said his dad. 'Just don't—'

Oliver finished his dad's sentence for him, ' ... get them mixed up with terrible danger. I won't, Dad, I promise.' Despite his sunny attitude, even Oliver thought he might cry at that moment, so he popped the sandwiches away in his pocket, hugged his dad and went aboard to welcome his crew.

***

Amy Zone, Stella X and Brumph were all waiting to greet Oliver when he arrived on the bridge.

'Hello, crew chums,' said Oliver.

'Morning, Captain,' said his crew, standing to attention.

'Now, for a start, there is no need to stand to attention for me,' said Oliver. 'I'd like to think I'm more of a friend than a captain, so from now on, I want you to call me Olly.'

'Olly?' said the crew.

'Olly Jolly,' said Oliver with a friendly smile.

'Yes, Captain,' said the crew.

Oliver wasn't sure what to make of that, so he just went on talking: 'Today, we set out on an adventure unlike any in history. It will be our job to spread harmony beyond the bounds of the known universe, to planets and civilizations no one from home has ever encountered before. Are there any questions?'

Stella put up a tentacle. 'These planets and civilizations,' she said, 'will we get to learn their languages?'

'We will,' said Oliver. 'It will be an important part of spreading harmony.'

'Including their rude words?' asked Stella.

'Well, I *suppose*,' said Oliver.

'That is pazzle-flurpingly vlacktastic news!' said Stella, using some of the very rudest words in the universe.

Oliver went bright red at the sound of them.

'And we're going to be facing all kinds of terrible danger, aren't we?' asked Amy.

'I don't know about "all kinds of terrible danger" as such,' said Oliver. 'We might encounter a bit of mild peril now and again, I suppose.'

'But there's at least a *chance* that we could get eaten?' asked Amy hopefully.

'Well, I *suppose*,' said Oliver.

'Yay!' said Amy, but Stella looked concerned.

'Not really,' Oliver whispered to Stella.

Amy wasn't listening – she was marching round the bridge chanting, 'I'm going to be a danger arranger – yippee!'

Amy was smiling, Stella was smiling and, for all Oliver knew, Brumph was smiling too. Oliver hoped that, with all this enthusiasm, he could make the mission a success. He wanted to show everyone on the Galactic Capital Planet that he wasn't useless after all.

'Righto then,' Oliver went on. 'Brumph, I presume you've checked our engines and we're ready for blast-off? Suffering Saturn, what is that awful smell?'

Stella grabbed Oliver and whispered urgently at him, 'That is how Brumph communicates, remember? Through funny-flavoured smells.'

'Oops!' said Oliver. 'Sorry, I forgot. What was he saying with that one?'

'Aye aye, Captain!' Stella translated.

'Excellent!' said Oliver, trying not to breathe through his nose. As Brumph headed off to the engine room, Oliver called out after him, 'You will make sure the air conditioning units are working at one hundred per cent efficiency at all times, won't you, Brumph?' He turned his attention back to the bridge. 'Well, I think it's time we all got to our … our, you know … um, chairs,' he said.

'Do you mean "stations", Captain?' asked Stella.

'That's exactly what I *do* mean,' said Oliver. 'So everybody, please put on your … um, seat belts.'

'Do you mean "stability harnesses", Captain?' asked Stella.

'Hmm,' said Oliver thoughtfully. He wasn't really listening any more. He was too busy looking over the control panel of the ship.

'Have you lost something, chief?' asked Amy.

'No, no,' said Oliver with a smile. 'I'm just looking for the … for the … '

'For the button that makes it go?' asked Amy.

'That's the one,' said Oliver.

'I'm going to take a wild guess here, Captain,' said Stella. 'You've never piloted a spaceship before, have you?'

'I've used the simulator billions of times,' said Oliver, 'but I've never actually tried out a real one, no.'

If any other crew had learned that their captain – and chief pilot – didn't actually know how to fly a spaceship, never mind a hugely powerful one that was going to blast them off to the farthest corner of the universe, they would have mutinied on the spot. But the crew of the *Some Hope* were young and enthusiastic and they didn't know any better. So instead of telling the captain to take a running jump and leaving immediately to join a gang of space pirates, Amy just pointed to the button that made the ship go.

'It's the green one,' she said. 'The one with the words "This Is The Button That Makes It Go" written on it.'

'Ah!' said Oliver. 'Yes, yes ... Just testing you, Amy. Well done.'

He was about to press the button when he looked out of the window and across to the observation platform of the spaceport. He could just about make out his dad – a tiny, faraway figure now – and he waved at him. The tiny, faraway figure waved back.

'I'll make you proud of me, Dad,' said Oliver under his breath. 'I promise I will.'

Oliver pressed the button. The engines flared and roared and, trembling with extraordinary power, the spaceship *Some Hope* shot straight backwards into the hangar bay it had just taxied out of.

'Help! We're going to crash!' cried Oliver. He had tried to keep his calm, but his calm had escaped and was now running around inside his brain, jibbering like a nervous wombat.

Amy slipped quickly out of her stability harness and rushed over to Oliver's station.

'Can we make it stop, please?' Oliver burbled. 'Really rather quickly, otherwise – oh dear!'

'Is this another test?' asked Amy.

'What?' burbled Oliver. 'Er, no!'

'Then you need to correct the directional guidance system!' yelled Amy.

'The what?' said Oliver, looking around wildly for whatever it was she was on about.

'The steering wheel!' said Stella.

'*Oh*,' said Oliver. 'Well, why didn't you *say* that?' he asked Amy.

'Turn the wheel before we plough right through the wall of the hangar bay!' cried Amy.

Oliver turned the wheel and the *Some Hope* stopped hurtling straight backwards.

Instead, it started hurtling straight forwards – in the direction of the observation deck of the spaceport, where Oliver's dad was standing. Oliver's dad, like everyone else on the observation deck, took one look at the massive spaceship that was suddenly hurtling towards him, screamed, and ran for his life.

The *Some Hope* missed the observation deck by a whisker and started gyrating crazily. It knocked the top off the control tower and smashed into the catering building, scattering inflight meals across a three-mile radius – where they remained completely uneaten by the local wildlife (animals will eat practically anything, but even animals have standards).

Brumph appeared on the bridge and let out another funny-flavoured smell.

Stella translated again: 'What in niggling Neptune is going on?'

'Is that really what he said?' asked Oliver.

'Well, no,' said Stella, 'what he actually said was a lot ruder than that, but that's what he meant.'

'Don't worry, Brumph, I've got the hang of it now,' said Oliver confidently, and he turned the wheel again. The *Some Hope* immediately flipped upside down. 'Ah. Maybe not,' Oliver said as he hung on to the steering wheel for dear life.

Eventually, Stella and Amy were able to make their way over to Oliver and help him turn the wheel correctly, and the ship righted itself.

'That's better,' said Oliver as he sat back down and straightened his uniform. 'I don't think anyone noticed that, did they?'

Down on the ground, ambulances and fire trucks sped to the rescue of the bystanders on the observation platform, their sirens screaming.

'That was amazingly dangerous,' said Amy. 'And we haven't even left yet! Cool!'

Oliver thought this might be a good time to change the subject. 'Anyone fancy a mint?' he asked.

'I think I'm going to be ill,' said Stella.

‘I didn’t know you got travel sick, Stella,’ said Oliver. ‘Poor you! I love a mint when I’m on a journey. Tell you what, I’ll leave the bag out in case you change your mind. Off we go!’

By some kind of miracle, Oliver managed to press the right button, pull the right lever and turn the right wheel. At last, with a colossal surge of power, the spaceship *Some Hope* went blasting off towards the very farthest corner of the universe.

Chapter 3
Friends I haven't met yet

'Captain's Diary,' said Oliver into his recording device in his most important-sounding voice. 'Space date – actually, I'm not sure what the date is. The calendar's gone funny. Hang on a sec, I'll give it a bang. Here we go. Oh dear. It's fallen off the wall and got the teeniest bit, um, smashed to pieces. Sorry, crew chums? Is there anyone who could possibly help me sort this out? What do you mean, I'm still recording? Oh yes, I am, aren't I? Oops. I just need to find the Off button, which is – where is it?'

At last, Oliver located the Off button and pressed it.

It was the first official day of the mission and things weren't going as well as he'd hoped.

For a start, the journey to the farthest corner of the universe hadn't been easy. The *Some Hope* was built to cover vast distances in next to no time. In the old days, it took centuries to travel to far-off planets and so spaceship crews had to be frozen for the journeys. Everyone hated that because you always woke up feeling like a bag of oven chips. As the years passed, ever more powerful rockets were developed that allowed ships to travel faster and faster. First there was Hyper-Drive, which meant that you could fly a billion miles in the time it took to eat lunch. Then there was Super-Hyper-Drive, which meant that you could fly a billion miles in the time it took to eat a light snack. Then Super-Dooper-Hyper-Drive which meant that you could fly a billion miles in the time it took to unwrap a chocolate bar.

The *Some Hope* went one better. It had the newly-developed Eek-Drive which meant that you could fly a billion miles before you even realized you were hungry.

The Eek-Drive – or, as it was originally called, the 'Eek!' Drive – got its name because you arrived at your destination so quickly that it always came as a bit of a shock. The two most important things about the Eek-Drive were that:

a) you waited till you'd cleared a planet's atmosphere before you engaged it, and
b) you made sure your ship was pointing in exactly the right direction. If it was just a few inches off, you would end up in a completely different part of the universe – and that could be rather annoying.

So if, say, your ship had just left the atmosphere of the Galactic Capital Planet, and the first mate was still calculating the exact coordinates of your destination (say, the farthest corner of the universe) when, say, the captain of your ship plonked, say, a bag of mints on, say, the button that engages the Eek-Drive and therefore, say, engaged the Eek-Drive by mistake, well … It was just as well that the first mate was as interested in danger as Amy Zone.

'OK,' Amy said. 'That's an interesting choice: engaging the Eek-Drive before we know where we're pointing so that we don't know where we're going and we might just end up in the heart of a supernova or a black hole – burned to a frazzle or squished flat.' She thought about that for a moment. '*Cool*!'

'Did I do that?' asked Oliver, and he quickly snatched up his bag of mints. 'Oops. Sorry.'

The rest of the almost impossibly quick journey, which took them across impossibly vast reaches of space and might have ended up in a supernova or a black hole, passed in anxious silence.

'Eek!' cried the crew when it had finished. 'That *was* quick!'

Oliver checked himself very carefully. When he was sure he hadn't been burned to a frazzle or squished flat, he took a look out of the window. 'Well, I'm pretty sure we're not in the heart of a supernova or a black hole.'

'But apart from that,' said Stella, 'we don't know where we are.'

'Which means we *could be* in the farthest corner of the universe,' said Oliver positively.

'We *could* be … ' said Amy, trying to sound hopeful.

'We could just as easily be in my auntie's back garden,' said Stella.

'Really?' said Oliver. He was looking out at a particularly desolate stretch of space. 'She's not much of a gardener, is she?'

'I'll run a scan and find out our exact location,' said Amy.

'Well, it certainly *looks* like the farthest corner of the universe,' said Oliver. 'I can't imagine there's much life on any of these barren rocks.'

'Captain, we're receiving a message,' said Stella.

'Really?' said Oliver. 'Are you sure it's not just a glitch?'

'It doesn't sound like a glitch,' said Stella. 'It sounds ... like a party.'

'What?' said Oliver. 'Can you play it through the speakers, please?'

Stella pressed a button and at once the bridge was filled with the clamour of a merrily chattering voice.

'What is it saying?' asked Oliver.

'I'm not sure – it's not a language I know,' said Stella. 'I'll try to patch it through the computer's translation algorithm and see what we get.'

'But those noises in the background,' said Oliver. 'They sound like laughter ... and dance music.'

'And people jumping into swimming pools,' said Stella. 'As I say, it sounds like a party.'

'I bet it's a trap,' said Amy. 'I mean, it sounds so lovely and friendly – but that's just to lure us in and the next thing we know, we'll be grabbed and basted and barbecued! At last, I'll get to be a danger arranger – yippee!'

'Barbecued?' Oliver sighed.

'Well, it is a party, after all. And being barbecued would be more interesting than being stuck on little cocktail sticks—'

'Amy,' Oliver continued patiently, 'I know you're on the lookout for excitement, but we have come here to spread peace, and we're not going to do that if we just think the worst of everyone before we've even met them. So – until we know better – it's not a trap, it's a party, OK?'

'Whatever you say, chief,' said Amy, but she didn't sound convinced.

'The computer's beginning to make some sense of the message,' said Stella. 'There will be certain words it'll get wrong, but we might be able to work out what they mean.'

'Hey – *wallpaper*!' crackled the voice from the speakers. 'We couldn't help noticing you are – *grand piano* – passing way, way close to this little – *hat stand* – that we call PARTY CENTRAL! So we were just – *egg juice* – if you guys wanted to join us – *hopscotch fudge segment* – party animals. We could even have – *spaniel frighteners*! Please say yes, it'll be – *umbrella*!'

'See?' said Oliver. 'And you said it might be a trap.'

'What does "spaniel frighteners" mean, though?' said Amy. 'It could still be a trap, chief.'

'I don't want to sound negative, Captain,' said Stella.

(For a moment, Oliver felt a pang that they still weren't calling him 'Olly Jolly' but he ignored it.) 'But Amy is right to be cautious. The message we've just heard – well, I can't be a hundred per cent certain that the translation was accurate … The computer was just doing its best to make sense of it. They sound friendly but they did say "we could even have spaniel frighteners". That might mean anything.'

'There's only one way to find out,' said Oliver. 'I'll get Brumph to prepare the shuttle, and we'll pop down and have a look for ourselves.'

'Yay!' said Amy. 'We're going to jump right into a trap!'

***

They left Brumph in charge of the ship, got into their spacesuits and flew down to the planet.

Oliver didn't want Amy or Stella talking about traps so he suggested they play a game of 'I Spy'.

'I spy with my little eye, something beginning with T,' said Amy.

'Ooh, that's a good one,' said Oliver encouragingly. 'Erm … toes? No, you can't really see them in these space boots. Tonsils? No, again, they're tucked away. I know – teeth!'

'No,' said Amy.

'Tongue?' said Oliver.

'No,' said Amy.

'Tentacles?' said Stella. Being an octopod, she was very proud of her tentacles.

Oliver had a thought and his heart sank. 'It's not a trap, is it?'

'No,' said Amy.

'Well, that's something at least,' said Oliver.

Amy continued, 'It's "Three People Who Are Flying Straight Into A Trap". Yippee!'

Oliver gave Amy a disappointed look.

'We're coming in to land,' said Stella, 'so each of us should take one of these earpieces. They're connected to the ship's computer and will try to translate what the locals say to us. The more they say, the faster the ship will learn their language, and the more we'll understand what they really mean.'

They put their earpieces in just as the shuttle touched down. Despite his positive attitude, Oliver couldn't help being a little concerned. What if Amy was right, and it *was* all a trap? What if, when the shuttle doors opened, they found themselves faced not with a crowd of happy party animals but with a horde of sneaky monsters? It didn't help that Amy was clearly very excited by the possibility that they were about to be turned into party food. Oliver took a deep breath, pressed the button and the shuttle doors hissed open.

'Oh look, little green men!' said Amy.

'And women,' added Oliver.

'Little green *party animals*, you mean,' said Stella.

The shuttle was indeed surrounded by little green party animals with big round bellies, wearing brightly-coloured shirts and shorts and party hats. At the sight of Oliver and his crew, the party animals cheered joyfully. As far as the eye could see, there were tables with food laid out, bands playing, bouncy castles, trampolines and swimming pools.

'See?' said Oliver. 'It's a party.'

'Traps don't look like traps,' said Amy. 'Or they wouldn't be traps.'

But before Oliver could try to persuade her otherwise, the party animals clustered around them, draping garlands of beautiful flowers around their necks and handing them glittering drinks in large, hollowed-out nutshells.

'This looks yummy!' said Oliver and he took a long sip.

'Might be poison,' said Amy. 'How exciting! I wonder if it kills this plant!' and she poured hers all over a plant, which, disappointingly for her, did not die.

Oliver stepped quickly in front of Amy, hoping that no one would see what she'd done. 'Good afternoon,' he announced. 'We are a mission sent from the Ministry of Universal Harmony back home at the heart of the universe. Take us to your leader.'

An especially round and smiling party animal strode up to them through the crowd. 'No need for all that – *fence post arithmetic* – my friends,' he said. The ship's computer was still having problems translating some of the words the party animal used, but Oliver recognized his voice as the one from the message.

'I'm Slemm Gassplants,' the party animal went on, 'and I'm here to bid you welcome to this – *cockatoo abacus* – day of fun, partying and, now you're here – *spaniel frighteners*!'

'And what do you mean by "spaniel frighteners" exactly?' said Stella.

'*Spaniel frighteners* means ... well, *spaniel frighteners*,' said Slemm Gassplants with a smile. 'Sorry, but it's very difficult to explain if you don't have the right – *vim catastrophe* – word.'

'It might just be a very rude word,' said Stella.

'It might just be a trap,' said Amy.

'It might just mean spaniel frighteners,' said Oliver. 'Has no one considered that?'

'I can't see any spaniels,' said Amy. 'And who would want to frighten one if there were any?'

'We're a very lucky bunch of – *four-door hatchbacks* –

here on planet Party Central,' explained Slemm, 'so every six or seven – *coffee tables* – we join together to give thanks for all the wonderful – *mayonnaise* – that life has given us. Any time we're – *giddy ostrich confusion* – enough to be joined by some – *gravel akimbo* – such as yourselves, well, we're only too happy to have you join the party, and have a special – *spaniel frighteners* – moment. So please come and have some fun!'

'What did I tell you, Amy?' said Oliver. 'It's a party. Whatever "spaniel frighteners" means, it's something good.' Somehow, though, he couldn't help feeling a tiny bit disappointed. After all, he'd crossed vast reaches of space to spread the message of peace and now he'd got here, he'd discovered that they were already *at* peace. In fact, as far as he could work out, Slemm and the rest of the party animals had never even *heard* of war. Of course, Oliver was glad they were happy, but he did feel like he'd wasted his time.

'I suppose we could leave a phone number if they ever fancied popping over to our end of the universe for a cup of tea and a biscuit, but that's about all we can do here,' he told Amy and Stella, sadly.

'Cheer up, chief,' said Amy brightly. 'We've only just got here. You never know, this could still turn out to be a trap.' She grabbed Stella and together they went off looking for terrible danger.

***

Left on his own, Oliver spent the rest of the day eating delicious food and finding out as much as he could about life on Party Central. Unsurprisingly, parties were the focus of everything. Slemm explained that their year was divided into three months. The months were called: 'Getting Ready To Have A Party', 'Having A Party' and 'Not Bothering To Clean Up After The Party Because, Before You Know It, There'll Be Another Party So What's The Point? Besides I Feel Bad Because I Ate Too Much Cake And I Really Need To Lie Down.'

'Your months have very long names,' said Oliver.

'That's the – *stem ginger patio doors* – why there are only three of them,' said Slemm. 'There's no room on a calendar for any more! But we're being far too – *faster ocelot pow pow* – and the band has just started my favourite tune. Come with me and I'll teach you a dance that you are going to – *kitchen explosion* – till your feet hurt. Come to think of it, those boots might be a problem.'

Oliver agreed that he couldn't dance in his heavy space boots, so he took them off and put on a pair of party shoes. Slemm was quite right about the dance: Oliver loved it. He got so hot dancing in his spacesuit that he took that off and went for a splash in one of the pools to cool down. When he got out of the pool, a kindly party animal told him that his spacesuit had been sent for cleaning.

'It was a bit – *disastrous hosepipe*!' said the party animal. Even though the ship's computer hadn't been able to translate exactly what he meant, Oliver understood by the way the party animal wrinkled his nose.

'Would you mind wearing some party clothes instead?' the party animal asked. 'Only until your suit is completely – *venomous hamster* – of course.'

'You're all a bit smaller than me,' said Oliver. 'I'm not sure you'd have any clothes that would fit me.'

'They will fit you like a – *sleek butterscotch* – don't worry,' said the party animal and he showed Oliver into a changing room.

The brightly-coloured shirt and pair of shorts he'd been given must have been made for an exceptionally large party animal because they did indeed fit Oliver like a – *sleek butterscotch* – glove. They were even big enough to fit Oliver's big round belly. Oliver didn't remember having a big round belly before they landed on the planet.

'I suppose it's because of all that delicious food they've been giving me,' he said to himself.

He put on the party hat and was about to leave when he caught sight of himself in the mirror. For a moment, he didn't recognize his own reflection. The party clothes suited him so well, it was almost as if he belonged here on this planet.

Almost as if he'd never worn any other kinds of clothes ...

Oliver shivered at the thought, then he shook his head. He was being silly. It was Amy and her obsession with traps that was making him worry needlessly.

Besides, there was no time for such unhappy thoughts – Slemm Gassplants was waiting for him outside the changing room.

'At last!' Slemm cried. 'It's time for – *spaniel frighteners*!'

***

Slemm led Oliver over to where hundreds of party animals were already seated at long tables. Oliver could see that "spaniel frighteners" obviously meant some kind of feast – but he couldn't see what the main course was going to be.

The moment they saw him, the party animals rose to their feet and cheered. Oliver knew he should be grateful that they were being so kind to him, but he couldn't help feeling a bit scared too. He was shown to an empty seat at the head of the table. On either side of him were Stella and Amy. They were now wearing party animal clothes too and they were both smiling.

'Hello, chief!' said Amy. 'Have you had a good afternoon? Because we have!'

'Did you find out that this is actually a trap after all?' said Oliver.

'No!' laughed Amy. 'I couldn't have been more wrong: the party animals are a peaceful, friendly people.'

'So you don't think they're going to barbecue us, then?' asked Oliver.

'Why would they bother barbecuing yucky old us, when they can make food as tasty as this?' asked Stella as she reached out with her tentacles to give Oliver a bowl of thick green goo. 'You've got to try it – it's delicious.'

Oliver took the bowl but he didn't try the green goo. 'I don't understand,' he said. 'What persuaded you?'

'Well, for a start, we found out that they do my favourite thing here: Extreme Sports,' said Amy. 'Only because this is Party Central, they're Extreme Party Games. I've played Extreme Pass The Parcel, Extreme Musical Statues and Extreme Pin The Tail On The Donkey. They're just like ordinary party games, except you're in a volcano. It was a bit hot down there, so we changed out of our spacesuits.'

'And I have learned so many new rude words,' said Stella happily. 'Merciful Mercury, they've got a lot of them.'

'As a matter of fact,' said Amy, 'Stella and I were just beginning to think we might want to stay on here for a bit – isn't that right, Stella?'

'Yes, please!' said Stella.

Oliver looked at Amy and Stella. The party animal clothes fitted them just as perfectly as they fitted him. He noticed that they, too, had grown big round bellies. *From eating all this thick green goo, no doubt*! thought Oliver. *And now they want to stay here forever*?

At that moment, Oliver realized what "spaniel frighteners" had to mean. The party animals weren't going to eat them – oh no! What they had planned was far worse! Oliver had a vision of people landing on this planet before now – maybe other Space Mistakes, the other young people who'd been sent out here by the Wise Brains. The party animals would welcome them, find a way of getting them to change into party animal clothes, swell their bellies with party animal food and slowly but surely ... *turn them into party animals*! He looked at the green smiling faces all around him. Who knew how many of them had been lured to this planet, only to be taken over, transformed and turned into party animals at this rather sinister ceremony called "spaniel frighteners"!

It *was* a trap after all!

Look at Amy and Stella, he thought. *They're halfway to being taken over already. They dress like party animals, they eat like party animals, they even laugh like party animals.*

All they need now is to change the colour of their skins to green and they will become *party animals! There'll be nothing left of the original Amy and Stella. When the next ship lands, they'll just be green party animals smiling their silly heads off – and so will I.*

Oliver looked down. He saw with a jolt of pure terror that his thumbs had gone green!

'Noooooooo!' he screamed and sprang to his feet. It had already started. The green would soon cover his hands, then his arms and then the rest of him, he would shrink down to party animal size, he would forget who he was and where he came from – and then it would be as if Oliver Jolly had never existed!

Everyone around Oliver was staring at him.

'Amy! Stella!' he barked commandingly. 'We're leaving!'

'What are you on about, chief?' Amy asked.

'Now!' said Oliver. 'That's an order!' He started marching purposefully towards the shuttle.

Amy and Stella looked at one another. 'What's he so worked up about?' asked Stella as they hastened after him.

Slemm Gassplants called out to them, 'You can't go now. You're going to miss it!' He pointed to a huge tray that was being carried towards the long tables by twenty of the strongest party animals. On the tray sat the largest – and the scrummiest-looking – chocolate cake in the universe.

He went running after Oliver, pointing at the tray. 'Look – *spaniel frighteners*!'

'I'll "spaniel frighteners" you, you wretch!' snapped Oliver. 'Kidnapping innocent people and brainwashing them and turning them into little green party animals.' He grabbed Slemm by the scruff of the neck and marched him over to the cake.

'Don't, Captain! Please!' cried Amy.

But it was too late. Oliver pushed Slemm's face right into the cake. The party animals carrying it were so shocked, they gasped.

'What have you done?' said Amy.

'That chocolate cake is sacred to the party animals,' said Stella. 'As well as being the scrummiest in the universe, apparently. This is a terrible insult.'

'Not another word!' said Oliver. 'You can thank me later.'

Amy and Stella looked back at the party animals. Their mood had clearly changed. Instead of happy, smiling faces, they were now frowning angrily. A few had got to their feet. Some were even running towards Oliver, waving their fists and shouting.

'They're using all their *very* rudest words,' said Stella. 'That's interesting.'

'And I do now feel like we're in the tiniest bit of danger – which I love, obviously,' said Amy.

'Oh, and they've just declared *sponge* on us,' said Stella. 'The computer can't quite translate that word, but I'm pretty sure it's going to turn out to be *war*.'

'Well, at least now they'll need someone to come here and spread peace,' said Amy, after they'd started running back to the shuttle.

'Yes,' said Stella. 'There's quite a lot of them running after us, you know. I think we should run faster.'

***

Oliver, Amy and Stella got to the shuttle seconds before the rather large and very angry mob of party animals caught up with them. When they had cleared the planet's atmosphere and were heading back to the *Some Hope*, Oliver explained about the whole terrible ritual of "spaniel frighteners".

'You think they were going to turn us into party animals?' said Amy.

'Yes,' said Oliver. 'The rotters.'

'By lending us their clothes because it was too hot for ours?' said Stella.

'And by giving us big round bellies,' said Oliver.

'Because their party animal food was so nice?' said Amy.

'That's it,' said Oliver. He got the feeling that they were not convinced.

‘So you think they were trying to turn us into party animals because they were kind and generous, and they gave us everything we wanted without asking for anything in return,’ said Stella. ‘That certainly sounds like a fiendish plan by a malevolent race of aliens to me.’

‘You said you wanted to stay on there for a bit!’ said Oliver. ‘That was them beginning to control your minds. Soon enough, you’d have forgotten who you were.’

‘We wanted to stay on there because of the fun we were having,’ said Amy.

‘And the good weather, nice food and friendly company,’ said Stella.

‘Ah,’ said Oliver. His fear of the party animals was giving way to a much deeper and more terrible fear – the fear that he might just have made a complete twerp of himself.

‘Wait a moment, though!’ he said. ‘What about my thumbs? They’ve gone green. Are you seriously telling me that they weren’t about to change the colour of our skins?’

‘Your thumbs went green,’ said Amy, ‘because you put them in the bowl of thick green goo. I don’t think the colour is permanent.’

Oliver sucked one of his thumbs. The green colour started coming off. Oh yes, and it tasted *delicious*.

'I suppose we could just pop back and explain that it was all a bit of a misunderstanding,' said Oliver.

'No chance,' said Stella. 'Not now they've declared *sponge* on us.'

'We'd be lucky if they didn't barbecue us now,' said Amy.

'Oh look,' said Stella, pointing at the shuttle's main screen. 'The ship's computer has finally translated "spaniel frighteners" and ... it means *big feast to welcome our brand new best friends with the largest – and the scrummiest – chocolate cake in the universe*.'

Oliver was inconsolable. This was the second time he had nearly caused a war, armed only with some cake.

When they got back to the ship, he went straight to his cabin and locked the door. By his bedside he kept the cheese and pickle sandwiches that his dad had given him the day he left. He wanted to run over and rip the packet open and eat them because he knew the taste would remind him of home and comfort. Then he remembered what his dad had said: 'You never know when they might come in handy.'

There would be a time when he would need them.

There would be a time when he would learn from all the mistakes he kept making, and do some good.

Chapter 4
Galactic evilness

The spangly black Vespidrillion battleship glittered against the spangly black backdrop of space. On its bridge, Gloth – the dark lord of the Vespidrillion Empire – stared out into the universe.

'Soon,' he growled, 'all of this will be mine. Every creature on every planet will kneel before me and the might of my Vespidrillion battlefleet. We shall ride to supreme power on a tide of war and destruction. The tears of the conquered will flow like rivers into a swamp of misery ... ' Gloth stopped and thought for a moment. 'Into a *sea* of misery? Yes, that sounds better.' He cleared his throat and started again, 'The tears of the conquered will flow like rivers into a sea of—'

Before he could finish, the door swooshed open and Vlort – his second-in-command – marched into the room.

'Your Galactic Evilness,' said Vlort, bowing his head and giving the Vespidrillion salute, which involved sticking two fingers up your nose and making a squeaking noise.

'How many times have I told you? Don't interrupt me when I'm doing The Speech!' snapped Gloth.

'What speech?' asked Vlort.

'You know perfectly well what speech,' said Gloth. 'The one about how every creature on every planet is going to kneel before me and the tears of the conquered will flow like rivers into—'

'A swamp of misery, yes,' said Vlort. 'I've been thinking about that and I've had an idea. Why not call it a *sea* of misery instead? I mean, after all, rivers flow into seas, don't they?'

'That's what I was *just about* to do!' said Gloth. 'Only you came barging in so I didn't have a chance.'

'There's no need to be like that – I was only trying to help,' sniffed Vlort.

'I know,' said Gloth. 'I'm sorry.'

'Well, carry on with your speech then,' said Vlort coldly, folding his arms. 'Don't mind me.'

Gloth shook his head and tried to get back into the right mood, but it was no good.

'What's the matter now?' asked Vlort.

'I've lost my place, haven't I?' said Gloth. 'Thanks a bunch! It was all going brilliantly. I had us riding to supreme power on a tide of war and destruction and now I can't remember where the swamp of misery bit goes.'

'*Sea* of misery,' corrected Vlort.

Gloth glowered at him.

'Well, now you've stopped,' said Vlort, changing the

subject, 'how about you and I go through some of these possible designs for our henchmen's uniforms?'

'Must we?' sighed Gloth wearily.

'Yes, we must!' said Vlort. 'We're just a start-up evil empire with – as yet – only one second-hand battleship and no uniforms for our henchmen to wear. As we speak, those poor henchmen are sitting around in their underwear, fuming. You can't expect trained henchmen to conquer the universe in string vests and pants, you know! They need shiny boots and helmets and scary-looking battle armour.'

'All right, all right,' said Gloth.

'That stuff takes ages to make,' said Vlort. 'I rang the customer service robot at Threads of Dread – you know, the company that's made uniforms for every evil empire of the last three million years? They say it will take at least six months to make us enough uniforms. That means we won't be able to take over the universe until the middle of March – at the earliest.'

'Can't the henchmen just dress in spangly black?' said Gloth. 'The same colour as the battleship?'

'I was going to talk to you about that as well,' said Vlort.

'Oh, come on!' said Gloth. 'We're evil, so our battleship *has* to be black – that's the rule.'

'*Spangly* black?' said Vlort. 'Against the *spangly black* backdrop of space?'

'Yes,' said Gloth.

Threads of Dread

are proud to present our autumn collection

Frogmar the Fiendish is wearing the sensational new conquerors' cape. Made from durable materials, it offers the combination of vim and vileness that our customers have come to expect.

Call us now to get your hands, tentacles, flippers, claws and robot clutching devices on designs that are out of this world!

Find us at Quadrant 33/9 Sector 91/beta Subsector 5.896.

Being bad has never looked SO good!

'But if our battleship is the same colour as what's behind it,' said Vlort, 'no one can see us!'

'Exactly,' said Gloth. 'It's camouflage! It gives us the element of surprise!'

'It gives us the element of getting bumped into all the time,' said Vlort.

'We do not get bumped into *all the time*,' said Gloth.

'We get bumped into an awful lot,' said Vlort. 'Don't you see how bad it looks for us? We say we're going to conquer the universe and then some passing spaceship comes tootling along and bumps into us, apologizes by saying they didn't see our battleship until it was too late and then suggests we paint it a different colour to avoid it happening again.'

'But black is a really cool colour!' said Gloth.

'Is it cool to have to spend all that money at the Evil Space Garage to get the dents out?' said Vlort.

'Yes!' said Gloth crossly, even though he knew it wasn't. 'I don't care what you say,' he went on, 'I am not painting my battleship pink!'

'I never said pink. Orange would be just as good, or a nice lilac.'

'Lilac? Why stop there? Why not put some stripes on it and make it look like an evil galactic ice lolly?'

'Now you're just being silly.'

Before they could go on with their row, the door swooshed open again and one of their henchmen marched in, glowering furiously. The henchmen had waited so long for uniforms to wear that they'd run out of clean underpants of their own and were now having to wear their grannies' underwear instead. This particular henchman's pair was especially large and frilly.

'My lord,' said the henchman grimly, hoping that Gloth and Vlort wouldn't notice his unusual attire, 'we have just sighted a ship moving into this quadrant. From our initial observations, it looks like it might have the Eek-Drive.'

'The Eek-Drive?' said Gloth, and his eyes glittered. 'If we could capture a ship that powerful, we could use it to blast our way to the heart of the universe in next to no time. Imagine it, Vlort. Instead of hanging around here in the farthest corner, getting bumped into by puny fools, we could conquer all of space at a stroke! Henchman, prepare your troops.'

'But we don't have any uniforms, Your Galactic Evilness,' said the henchman, 'and I'm certainly not attacking anyone looking like *this*.'

'Silence!' roared Gloth. 'Do as I say or I will have you crushed into space dust!'

'Whatever!' said the henchman, and he marched out.

Gloth smiled. 'The moment of glory is at hand,' he said. 'Vlort, set us on an attack course.'

'What, now?' said Vlort. His arms were still full of colour charts and designs for henchmen uniforms.

'Yes, now!' said Gloth. 'Or do I have to do everything myself?'

'No, no, I'll do it!' said Vlort, looking around for somewhere to put his designs so he'd have his hands free.

'Excellent, excellent,' growled Gloth. Vlort punched the coordinates into the computer, and the engines of the Vespidrillion battleship roared into life.

'We ride to conquest and to glory!' cried Gloth. 'I think it might be time for an evil laugh. Mwa ha ha ha ha!'

***

The crew of the *Some Hope* had noticed the Vespidrillion battleship at much the same time as it had noticed them. Stella called Oliver to the bridge.

'Hello, Stella,' said Oliver. 'What can I do for you? No, don't tell me. It's time for a cup of tea, isn't it?'

After the unfortunate "spaniel frighteners" incident, Oliver had been doing everything he could to make his crew like him again. Every chance he got, he baked them cakes, told them jokes and made sure they never went too long without a nice hot drink inside them.

'No thank you, Captain,' said Stella.

'How about something fizzy?' said Oliver. 'A space cola, perhaps, or a star soda?'

'Honestly, Captain,' said Stella, 'that's not why I called you—'

'Biscuit?' said Oliver. 'Come on, you've been working very hard all morning. You deserve a biscuit.'

'Oh, all right then,' said Stella. She was feeling a bit peckish.

'Chocolate or raisins?' said Oliver.

'I really don't mind,' said Stella. 'Look, this is really rather urgent.' When she realized Oliver was just going to stand there with a tin of biscuits in each hand until she picked one, she said, 'Oh, raisins, please.'

'Good choice,' said Oliver. 'I love both of them, and so it's impossible for me ever to make up my mind which to have. Thank you for deciding for us both, Stella.' He took a bite of raisin biscuit. 'Yum!'

'*Anyway* ... ' said Stella, 'the reason I've asked you here is that we have been spotted by an enemy battleship.'

'How many times do I need to tell you?' said Oliver. 'We promised we wouldn't use that word, didn't we?'

'I'm sorry, Captain,' said Stella. 'We have been spotted by a *friend I haven't met yet* battleship.'

'That's better,' said Oliver. 'Where?'

‘I’ll put it up on the main screen for you,’ said Stella. She pressed a button and the huge display screen, which covered a whole wall of the bridge, flickered into life. A beautifully detailed star chart of the local area appeared.

‘Quadrant 33/9, Captain,’ Stella replied.

Oliver looked at the screen. ‘Can’t see it,’ he said.

Stella enlarged the image to help him. ‘Sector 91/alpha, Captain,’ she said.

Oliver looked at the screen a bit harder. ‘Nope, still nothing,’ he said.

Stella enlarged the image a little more. ‘Subsector 4.387, binary ecliptic,’ she said.

Oliver looked at the screen even harder for quite a long time before he said, ‘*Where*?’

‘Plummeting Pluto!’ said Stella. She’d run out of scientific ways to describe it, and she couldn’t enlarge the image any more, so she just pointed at the screen with the tip of one of her tentacles and said, ‘*There.*’

‘But that’s just a bit of the spangly black backdrop of space,’ said Oliver.

‘With respect, Captain,’ said Stella, ‘please look again. If you concentrate, you’ll see something.’

Oliver stared at the screen until his eyes hurt and then suddenly he cried out, ‘Ohhhh! There’s a spangly black battleship *in front of* the spangly black backdrop of space!

Camouflage – now that's clever.'

'Clever?' snorted Amy, who had just come on to the bridge. 'If they don't watch out, people'll be bumping into them all the time.'

'Don't you know what this means?' said Oliver. 'It's another lovely alien race we can reach out to. We're being given a chance to make up for that whole dreadful "spaniel frighteners" business. Let's send them a friendly message and ask them over for flapjacks. I just made a delicious new batch.'

'What if they're preparing to attack?' said Amy. 'That would be *brilliant*.'

'They're not preparing to attack – they're just sitting there,' said Oliver.

'With their cannons pointed straight at us,' said Amy.

'Really?' said Oliver, and his eyes flickered for a bit while he tried to think of a good reply. 'Ah,' he barked, when he'd thought of one, 'but they haven't *fired* them at us, have they?'

Amy shrugged, 'All right, no. They haven't.'

'Ha!' said Oliver.

'They *have* just started broadcasting this message,' said Stella. She pressed a button on her workstation and Gloth's harsh voice roared from the speakers: 'To any who hear this: despair! Surrender immediately, or the glorious Vespidrillion Empire will crush you into space dust.'

'Yippee! We're going to be attacked!' said Amy.

'Maybe they're just in a bad mood,' said Oliver, 'and what is the best way to cheer someone up? Invite them over for flapjacks, of course,' and he pressed the communicator button on his station.

'No, Captain!' cried Stella, but it was too late.

'Hey guys,' said Oliver into the communicator. 'Couldn't help noticing you were over there chilling and just wondered if you fancied popping over. We have flapjacks!'

'What did you do that for?' asked Stella.

'We're here to spread peace,' said Oliver. 'If we get attacked, I'll take the blame.'

'If we get attacked,' said Amy, 'it is going to be better than the best Extreme Sport ever!'

'They've started moving,' said Stella. 'They're heading straight for us!'

'What did I tell you?' said Oliver. 'No one can resist my flapjacks.'

'Meddling meteors! I hope you're right,' said Stella.

They watched as the ship got nearer … and nearer … and nearer … and nearer … and nearer … and nearer …

And then Oliver said, 'It's taking ages, isn't it? I mean, they've been heading straight for us for about an hour and a half and they still look a long, long way off.'

'They do, don't they?' said Amy.

'I'll put the kettle on while we wait,' said Oliver.

Stella checked her instruments, but the readings didn't make any sense. 'That's really odd,' she said. 'I wonder if there's a problem somewhere.'

***

There was a problem all right, but it wasn't with anything aboard the *Some Hope*. It was the problem Vlort had been wanting to bring up with the dark lord Gloth ever since they decided to go into the evil empire business together. The trouble was, he could never seem to find the right moment. Now that they were heading straight for another ship on an attack course, Vlort decided he couldn't put it off any longer.

'Your Galactic Evilness?' said Vlort.

'What is it now?' roared Gloth. 'Can't you see I'm in the middle of something?'

'This plan of yours ... to capture the ship with the Eek-Drive and use it to blast our way to the heart of the universe?' said Vlort.

'That's the something I'm in the middle of,' said Gloth testily.

'I think there might be a problem with it,' said Vlort.

'Watch yourself, Vlort,' said Gloth. 'If you stand in the way of the ultimate triumph of the Vespidrillion

Empire, I will not hesitate to have you crushed into space dust!'

'Well, that's *charming*,' said Vlort. 'You do know I made that uniform you're wearing with my own hands? It took *weeks* – sewing on all the monstrous buttons, getting the villainous seams straight – but if I want to say something, I get my head bitten off.'

'Have you seen this communication we've just received from that ship?' said Gloth, waving a printout in Vlort's face. 'They've invited us over for flapjacks! This is going to be easier than I thought! Prepare to be crushed into space dust, you trusting fools!'

'On the subject of the trusting fools,' said Vlort. 'If we don't come up with a solution to this problem I'm talking about, there won't *be* any ultimate triumph of the Vespidrillion Empire.'

'I'm not listening,' said Gloth.

'But you have to listen,' said Vlort, 'or this precious attack of yours might turn out to be a teeny bit … embarrassing.'

'Not listening to a word,' said Gloth.

'Please, Your Galactic Evilness, you have to!' said Vlort.

Gloth put his fingers in his ears and made 'Nee-naw' sounds so he couldn't hear anything Vlort said.

And the Vespidrillion battleship roared onwards, heading straight for the *Some Hope* on an attack course.

***

Oliver came back to the bridge carrying a tray of cups and some flapjacks in a transparent box.

'They smell yummy, don't they?' he said. 'Right, what have I missed?'

'They're still heading straight for us on an attack course,' said Amy.

'What?' said Oliver, looking at the tiny black battleship on the screen. 'But they're still miles away. Have their engines conked out, do you think?'

Stella's huge brainy forehead was creased with worry as she tried to understand what was happening. 'That's just it, Captain,' she said. 'According to my instruments, they're less than five minutes away.'

'Then I need to get into my Extreme Sports gear!' cried Amy.

***

The Vespidrillion battleship was hurtling onwards, its battle cannons primed and ready to fire, its crew of evil henchmen waiting bad-temperedly in their underwear to storm aboard the *Some Hope*. Gloth and Vlort watched from the main screen on the bridge of the battleship as the *Some Hope* loomed in front of them, growing larger and larger by the moment. In only a few seconds' time, they would make contact, and the battle would commence.

***

At that exact same moment on the bridge of the *Some Hope*, Stella realized something.

'It's all going to be all right,' she said.

'Really?' said Amy, who had changed into sports kit, sweat bands and running shoes for the forthcoming attack.

'Come again?' said Oliver, who was hanging up a sign that said: 'Welcome, Friends We Haven't Met Yet!'

'I'm opening the airlock,' she said.

'I told you it would all be fine,' said Oliver.

'We're about to be attacked!' said Amy. 'Yippee!'

'We *are* about to be attacked,' said Stella, '*and* it's all going to be fine.'

***

The sight of the airlock door opening in front of his battleship made the dark lord Gloth wonder.

Surely, he thought, *it can't be this easy. This must be a trap.*

Then he remembered the invitation to pop over for flapjacks and he cackled with triumph.

'They're giving in!' Gloth shouted to Vlort over the roar of the engines. 'The puny fools are going to be crushed into space dust even sooner than I thought!'

Somewhere far, far at the back of Gloth's mind, down a dark alley of doubt, along a terrible terrace of trauma, at the end of an agonized avenue of anguish, a small weed of dread began to grow.

Maybe Vlort had been right about that pesky 'problem' all along.

But it was too late to think about that now.

***

'That's it,' said Stella. 'They're aboard. I'm going to close the airlock behind them. Shall we go and meet the new arrivals?'

'Excitement! Danger! Explosions!' cried Amy.

'No,' said Stella.

'Flapjacks?' said Oliver hopefully.

'As a matter of fact,' said Stella, 'your box of flapjacks is just what we need,' and she took the box from Oliver, opened it and emptied out all the flapjacks.

'Hey!' said Oliver.

'They're lovely flapjacks,' said Stella, 'but at the moment all I need is the box. Come on then, let's go and welcome them – or they'll think we have no manners.'

***

Oliver, Stella and Amy stood outside the airlock. Amy did some running on the spot to prepare herself for the excitement to come.

'You really don't need to do that,' said Stella.

'But they're in there, aren't they?' asked Amy.

Stella checked her instruments. 'Yes.'

'Then we're about to be attacked,' said Amy. 'I'm going to have to do lots of running and jumping to avoid the laser blasts and death rays.'

'*Well …* ' said Stella, but she didn't want to spoil the surprise. She pressed a button and the door of the airlock swooshed open. Oliver and Amy looked inside and saw …

Nothing.

'Eh?' they said.

'I thought you told us they were in here,' said Oliver.

‘They are,’ said Stella.

‘Where?’ said Amy.

‘It’s funny you should ask,’ said Stella. ‘It was the chief who gave me the idea, when he said they looked a long, long way off—’

Before Stella could go on Amy stopped her. ‘Can anybody else hear that horrible little whining noise?’ she said. ‘Like there’s a wasp or something trapped in here? There it is – hang on.’

Amy reached out to crush whatever it was that was making the noise but Stella very quickly shouted, ‘Don’t!’

‘Why not?’ Amy asked. ‘It’s only a wasp.’

‘No, it’s not,’ said Stella. She reached out with three of her tentacles and guided the thing that was not a wasp into the empty flapjack box and put the lid back on.

‘Look,’ she said, pointing into the box. Oliver and Amy had to squint, but they could just about see the Vespidrillion battleship, which was only the size of a large wasp, zooming angrily around inside.

‘They weren’t a long, long way off,’ said Stella. ‘They’re just very, very small.’

***

Aboard the battleship, there was chaos.

'We're tiny!' babbled the henchmen. 'You never told us we were tiny!'

'I didn't know,' said the dark lord Gloth.

'You had a pretty good idea,' said Vlort.

'No, I didn't,' said Gloth.

'I said there was a problem,' snapped Vlort. 'I believe my exact words were, "If we don't come up with a solution to this problem I'm talking about, there won't *be* any ultimate triumph of the Vespidrillion Empire."'

'Well, what about those other spaceships?' said Gloth crossly. 'The ones that kept bumping into us?'

'What do you think?' said Vlort. 'They're tiny too – just not quite as tiny as us. Living all your life in the farthest corner of the universe, you don't realize how small you are until you bump into something that's normal size.'

'Who says they're normal size?' said Gloth. 'If you ask me, *we're* normal size and they're unattractively enormous.'

'It doesn't really matter, does it?' said Vlort. 'Seeing as they are the ones who have just put us into a transparent box that very recently had ... ' he sniffed, 'of course, flapjacks in it.'

'The transparent box has not been made that can imprison the dark lord Gloth and the Vespidrillion Empire!' roared Gloth. 'Aim all firepower at the lid at once.'

The henchmen looked over at Vlort.

'Why not?' shrugged Vlort. 'It might be a laugh.'

So all the firepower of the Vespidrillion battleship was concentrated at the lid of the transparent flapjack box. In a sizzling blaze of multicoloured light, a salvo of destruction shrieked terrifyingly out of its battle cannons, heading straight for the lid of the box ... where it managed to make a tiny, sizzling black mark that didn't even go all the way through.

'Oh, bother,' growled Gloth.

***

'That's a thought,' said Stella when she saw the tiny black mark on the lid. 'I should make some airholes in the lid so they can breathe.' When she'd finished doing that, she popped the box in the stationery cupboard.

That should keep them from getting into any mischief, she thought.

***

Sitting in the darkness, among the boxes of paper, bottles of glue and rolls of tape, Gloth dreamed dark and terrible dreams, and plotted his revenge.

Chapter 5

The Surprise Machine

Three years passed. The *Some Hope* continued on its mission spreading peace to the farthest corner of the universe. After their disastrous meeting with the party animals and their surprising triumph over the Vespidrillion Empire, Oliver, Amy, Stella and Brumph started to get the hang of things. They encountered many kinds of strange alien races – including the jellyfish people of Splosh, the robot wizards of the moons of Spanglewand Prime and the skateboarding jungle monkeys of Radd – and made friends with them all. Stella learned a lot of new languages – and a huge number of rude words. Amy enjoyed all kinds of enormously dangerous adventures that the rest of the crew were too terrified to even think about. It was wonderful, but after three years, it was also a tiny bit ...

'Boring!' said Oliver on the bridge one morning.

'What is?' asked Stella.

'No,' said Oliver, 'I mean, it's not really boring, of course. It's amazing. The chance to travel to all these extraordinary planets and meet all these fascinating races of aliens without being *entirely* sure they're not going to eat us – it's terrific.

But it's also a teeny weeny bit—'

' … the same every time?' said Amy. 'I've been thinking that too. We find a planet, we land on it, we have an adventure and then we're back on the ship again in time for tea. It's not as exciting as it used to be.'

'A lot of the rude words I've been learning lately have been a bit too similar – and not nearly rude enough,' agreed Stella.

'Exactly,' said Oliver. 'I'd just like to be *surprised* once in a while. I don't care how. I just want something to happen that I'm not expecting.'

Then something happened that he wasn't expecting.

'Euw!' cried Oliver, pulling a face. 'What's that *awful* smell? Has the plumbing gone wrong again?'

Stella shot him a fierce look. 'That is not the smell of the plumbing,' she said. 'As you well know, Brumph, our highly respected engineer, communicates by giving off funny-flavoured smells. He can't help it – he's a superintelligent pot plant and that's what they do. If you say those smells remind you of the plumbing, it'll hurt his feelings.'

Oliver looked across at Brumph. Brumph was whizzing busily around in his plant pot with wheels on, fixing something. It didn't look like his feelings were hurt, but just in case, Oliver said, 'Sorry about that, Brumph. What did you say?'

There was another funny smell. Stella translated: 'He says he's fixing the plumbing. It's gone wrong again.'

Oliver didn't like people who said 'I told you so', so he didn't say 'I told you so'. Instead, he pointed at the screen and said, 'Now *that's* a surprise.'

'What is?' asked Amy.

'That planet, there,' said Oliver.

Amy and Stella looked over to where Oliver was pointing. On the screen, there was an arrow pointing at a tiny pinprick of light. Just above the arrow, the words 'Now *that's* a surprise' flashed on and off in bright red letters.

'I can't find it on any of the star charts,' said Amy.

Suddenly, a voice from behind them muttered, 'Yes, I'm sorry about that – it's my fault.'

The crew of the *Some Hope* jumped out of their seats – all of them, that is, except Brumph, who jumped out of his pot, which was quite a sight to see: the soil went everywhere.

Standing behind them was a mouse-like creature with blue fur. He was about five feet tall and stood upright. He was wearing brown overalls and three different pairs of spectacles. He had a screwdriver and was fiddling with a small device in one of his paws.

Then he did something even more surprising than suddenly appearing out of thin air. 'That's fixed it!' he said and suddenly disappeared back into thin air again.

The crew of the *Some Hope* looked round at one another. After a moment's thought, Oliver said the most intelligent thing any of them could think of to say, which was 'Ummm ... ?'

Before he could go on, the mouse-like creature reappeared.

'Now where was I?' said the mouse-like creature, his whiskers twitching thoughtfully. 'Oh yes, I remember: here.' He looked at the crew, changed his spectacles a couple of times, and said, 'Hello. I'm sorry, I'm experimenting with a new transportation device and there are a few teething problems. But never mind that now. My name is Banjax, and I am here for a very important reason, only I can't remember what it is.' Banjax twitched his whiskers thoughtfully again, but it didn't help him remember.

'Anyway,' he went on, 'it's nice to meet you.'

'Ummm ... ?' said Oliver again. It was still the most intelligent thing any of them could think of to say.

'Well, quite,' said Banjax. 'I'm an inventor, I think. Yes, I am. Of course I am, but I am also a bit ... '

'Forgetful?' suggested Stella.

'That's the one!' said Banjax. 'I'm a bit forgetful.' Then he stopped and thought for a moment. 'I'm sorry, I've forgotten what I was going to say.'

'You're an inventor,' said Amy. 'So what have you invented?'

'Oh, ah, I know this!' said Banjax. 'Well, um, lots of things. For a start, I invented that planet you've just noticed. I call it Burpleperherfenpursely.'

'Burple – ?' said Stella.

' … perherfenpursely,' said Banjax, helping her out. 'Silly name, I know, but we inventors like our privacy, so I thought if I invented a very small planet, and gave it a very big name, there wouldn't be enough space on any of the star charts to write the name and so the people who make the star charts would just ignore it.'

'You were right,' said Amy.

'Splendid,' said Banjax. 'So imagine my surprise when you lot appeared.'

'We were just passing,' said Stella. 'We didn't mean to ruin your privacy.'

'Oh, don't worry about that,' said Banjax. 'It's nice to have visitors now and again. In fact – I've remembered – that's why I popped up here.'

'Ummm … ?' said Oliver a third time. For someone who was only recently saying how much he wanted to be surprised, he was not dealing well with this surprising turn of events.

‘As well as the planet Burpleperherfenpursely,’ said Banjax, ‘my inventions include: strawberry flavoured rain, a talking earthquake, singing space trousers and … ’ he patted the pockets of his overalls, ‘well, and this little gizmo.’ He pulled out a short metal tube and handed it to Amy.

‘I call it an “Enlarging Tube”. If you look through this end, whatever’s at the other end becomes much bigger.’

Amy looked through the Enlarging Tube at the coffee cup she’d left on her workstation. She wasn’t in the least bit surprised to see that the coffee cup suddenly looked much bigger. She smiled kindly and handed the tube back to Banjax.

‘This is what we call a “telescope”. I’m afraid we already have them back where we come from,’ Amy told him. ‘They were invented thousands of years ago.’

‘“Telescope”, eh?’ said Banjax, shaking his head thoughtfully. ‘What a wonderful name! It’s so much better than “Enlarging Tube”. Ah well, that happens a lot when you’re an inventor. You think you’ve come up with something amazing and brilliant and it turns out someone else got there first. Thousands of years ago, you say?’

Amy noticed that Stella, Brumph and Oliver were all staring in the direction of her coffee cup. She looked round to see why and nearly fell over with surprise. It was huge – just as huge as it had looked through the telescope. Now it was Amy's turn to say 'Ummm ... ?'

'Is there a problem?' asked Banjax.

Amy was too stunned to answer, so Stella explained, 'That's not a telescope after all. When you look through a telescope, whatever's at the other end only *looks* much bigger. It doesn't actually *get* much bigger.'

'Then I *have* come up with something new,' beamed Banjax. 'Well, that's nice to know.'

'Yes, but how do we – ?' Amy began but she couldn't get to the end of her sentence. Instead, she just waggled her hand at the huge coffee cup.

' ... make it go back to the original size?' said Banjax. 'That's easy! You just turn the tube around and look through the other end.'

Amy did so and her coffee cup shrank back to its original size.

'Anyway,' said Banjax, 'the reason I came up here in the first place is that it's nice to have visitors now and again. Would you like to pop down to my workshop for a cup of tea? I've invented something new to go with it. I call them "biscuits". You can try one if you like.'

Banjax got everybody to hold hands and then he pressed the transportation device in his paw. At once, there was a flash of light, everyone felt like they were being tickled by very cold fingers and the next thing they knew, they were in Banjax's workshop.

Oliver looked around. He didn't want to say 'Ummm ... ?' again, so instead he said, 'Wow!'

'It's not bad, is it?' said Banjax. 'It saves all that time getting into a shuttle and flying to places.'

'I didn't mean your transportation device,' said Oliver, finding his voice at last.

'Oh,' said Banjax. 'Someone invented that thousands of years ago too, did they?'

'No,' said Oliver. 'Not at all. The transportation device is amazing.'

'I'm so pleased!' said Banjax, clapping his paws together with joy. 'I'm thinking of calling it the "Whoosh"! What do you think?'

'It's a very good name,' said Oliver, 'but the reason I said "Wow!" was because your workshop is just so wonderful.'

'Thank you,' said Banjax.

The workshop was huge – it looked like it went on for miles – and full of benches piled high with bits of machinery and computers, and blackboards all scribbled over with very complicated sums. Furnaces crackled and strange-looking robots trundled around assembling even stranger-looking machines.

'Welcome,' said Banjax, 'to Burpleperherfenpursely!'

***

The "biscuits" Banjax had invented turned out to be very much like the biscuits back home, only with more jam in them. He was very proud of them, so no one told him that they'd had biscuits back where they came from for thousands of years. When they had eaten enough to calm themselves down completely, Banjax took them on a tour of his workshop.

He showed them pens that did your work for you without you having to ask them, cups that refilled themselves the moment they were empty and helicopter hats that took you wherever you wanted to go without you even having to wake up first.

Then they passed a box about the size of a suitcase. There was a single red button on the top of it.

'What's that?' asked Oliver.

'That?' said Banjax, thinking for a moment. 'Oh! Yes! That is one of my few failed inventions – it's very sad. I call it the "Surprise Machine". I invented it about thirty years ago. My idea was that if you pressed the button, something really hugely amazingly surprising would happen. Well, the moment I finished it all those years ago, I pressed the button and … nothing happened.'

'Maybe that was the surprise,' said Amy.

'Maybe,' said Banjax. 'The funny thing is, I hadn't thought about it much since then, but this morning I camc across it and started tinkering with it again. It still doesn't work.'

Banjax twitched his whiskers thoughtfully for a moment, then he went wandering off ahead of them.

Before Oliver could follow him, Stella grabbed him and whispered, 'That must have been exactly the same time that we were on the bridge saying how bored we were, and how much we wanted to be surprised.'

'And then we spotted Burpleperherfenpursely,' said Oliver. 'Which *was* a bit of a surprise, wasn't it?'

'So perhaps it works after all,' said Amy. '*Awesome*!'

There was suddenly a funny-flavoured smell.

'Brumph's just thought of something,' said Stella. 'He says that if Banjax invented the Surprise Machine about thirty years ago and he pressed the button so that a really hugely amazingly surprising thing would happen—'

' … then maybe that thing *did* happen, only it didn't happen here, it happened back home, in the heart of the universe!' said Oliver.

'And the surprise was the sudden outbreak of peace!' said Amy. 'Good thinking, Brumph!'

‘It was certainly a surprise,’ said Stella. ‘No one’s ever really explained it.’

There was another funny-flavoured smell.

‘Brumph’s just thought of something else,’ said Stella. ‘If Banjax created peace back home by pressing the button on the Surprise Machine, then the next time someone presses the button, they could just as easily start another war.’

‘Good thinking, Brumph,’ said Oliver. ‘We can’t just leave this machine here then, can we? We’ll have to take it with us and put it somewhere safe so that no one will ever press that button.’

He tried to think of a good place, but he couldn’t concentrate because the funny-flavoured smell was lingering in the air. ‘What has Brumph been eating?’

‘Manure,’ said Stella.

‘Lovely,’ said Oliver.

***

Eventually, the tour of Banjax’s workshop came to an end.

‘You must come and visit us in the heart of the universe someday,’ said Stella. ‘I’m sure all these wonderful inventions of yours would be very popular back there.’

‘That’s so kind,’ said Banjax, ‘though to tell you the truth, I just like making things. Once they’re finished, I’m not really interested in what happens to them. I go on to something else. If there's anything you'd like to take with you, please do.'

'There is one thing ... ' said Oliver.

Banjax couldn't understand why they would want to have one of his few failed inventions.

'The Surprise Machine? Really?' he said. 'Well, I suppose it saves me the time and bother of throwing it away,' he added, 'but why don't you pick something that actually *works*?'

'It's difficult to explain,' said Stella. 'But trust us, this is a very kind gift.'

'Very well then,' said Banjax and he used his transportation device to send them back to the bridge of the *Some Hope*.

Despite hours of thinking about it, they couldn't decide where to put the Surprise Machine. In the end, Oliver just decided to leave it next to the hot chocolate machine on the bridge.

'I'm sure we'll be able to think of the right place tomorrow, but it's been a long – and surprising – day, and it's high time we all turned in,' he yawned.

He was the last to leave the bridge. He had engaged the computer autopilot to steer the ship through the night and he was about to turn the lights off when he noticed that

Banjax had left his Enlarging Tube behind. Would Banjax want it back? He was too tired to think about it now. So he picked it up and put it in the stationery cupboard for safekeeping.

It won't come to any harm there, thought Oliver, and he forgot all about it.

Chapter 6
Space Mistakes

The refridgy-fresh packet of cheese and pickle sandwiches still lay by Oliver's bedside. For over three years now, he had not eaten them because his dad had told him that they might come in handy sometime. That time had never come, and Oliver's tummy was rumbling. He grabbed the packet – which had kept the sandwiches as 'refridgy-squidgy' as the day they were made – and was about to tear it open when the speaker above his head crackled into life.

'Captain, there's a message for you from the ship's computer,' said Stella's voice.

Oliver put the packet of sandwiches in his pocket and headed off to the bridge.

A loud beeping greeted Oliver as he arrived on the deck. It was coming from the ship's computer. He pressed a button and the beeping stopped. The computer was warning him to correct the course of the ship or it would soon crash into a small planet.

Oliver started calculating the change in flight vectors, but then he caught sight of the main screen. It was showing the star field they were passing through. It was a particularly beautiful stretch of space, with purple nebulae and golden galaxies blazing and wheeling all around them.

'What was the message from the computer?' asked Stella.

'What?' said Oliver, completely lost in the beauty of space. 'Message?'

Brumph released a funny-flavoured smell.

'Oh, yomping Uranus, Brumph, you're right!' said Stella. 'We're about to crash into that small planet!'

'Oh, ah, yes,' said Oliver suddenly. He shook his head and went back to his calculations but he was so flustered that he got in a muddle.

'*I'll* do it,' said Stella crossly.

Brumph released another funny-flavoured smell.

'Yes, I *know* it's going to be very close,' said Stella, as she clacked frantically at her keyboard with five of her eight tentacles.

The small planet loomed larger and larger until it filled the screen. Oliver and Brumph both scrunched themselves up in anticipation of the impact.

'Hold on tight, you two!' Stella called out, clipping herself into her safety harness. The ship tilted sharply, sending pens and cups and plates – and anything else that wasn't nailed down – flying across the bridge, but they managed to avoid the planet by the narrowest of margins.

'That was close!' said Oliver once the ship had levelled out again. 'Well done, Stella.'

Amy came running on to the bridge. 'What just happened? I was doing two hundred press-ups – you know, just for fun – and suddenly I was on the ceiling.'

'It was my fault,' said Oliver, but before he could go on, the bridge was filled with more loud beeping.

'Is that another message from the computer?' asked Oliver.

A second loud beeping joined the first, and then another, and another – each at a slightly different pitch. Pretty soon, it sounded like a chorus of robot wasps was trying to sing the worst song in the universe very loudly.

Stella checked her instruments. 'Captain, these are distress beacons.'

'What?' asked Oliver, deafened by the ever-increasing noise of beeping.

'*Distress beacons*,' Stella said more clearly. 'You know, the thing you turn on when you crash, so that someone will know where you are and will come and rescue you.'

'Well – they're – jolly – loud,' yelled Oliver, as the sound of more and more distress beacons filled the air. 'Can – you – turn – the – noise – off – please?'

Stella pressed a button and the bridge fell silent again.

'Thank you,' said Oliver. He looked at the screen, which was still dominated by the surface of the small planet. They had narrowly avoided crashing into it, but a whole host of other ships clearly hadn't. Their wrecks dotted the planet like flies on a windscreen.

'What happened here?' asked Oliver.

'Maybe they were so busy enjoying the view of space, they didn't do their calculations in time,' said Stella. Oliver thought it wise to ignore her.

'The funny thing is,' Amy added, looking more closely at the screen, 'that all these ships seem to have come from back home. I thought *we* were the only mission to the farthest corner of the universe.'

Oliver had never told his crew about the Space Mistakes – all the other young men and women like him who had made a dreadful mess of something back home, and had been sent out here to the farthest corner of the universe. Now would have been a good time, but Oliver was worried that they'd lose all their respect for him if they found out he'd accidentally brought the universe to the brink of all-out war armed only with a blueberry muffin, so instead he said, 'Let's get down there and rescue them, shall we?'

They left Brumph in charge of the ship, and Oliver, Stella and Amy took the shuttle down to the planet's surface. They checked the wreckage of each crashed ship but there was no one in any of them.

'Well, where are all the pilots now?' asked Amy. 'Ooh, do you think they've been eaten? That means we might get eaten too! At last, some proper danger!'

'They haven't been eaten,' said Oliver, but even he wasn't entirely sure about that.

'They went looking for shelter,' said Stella. 'Look, there are some boot tracks leading away from this ship.'

'And from this one,' said Amy.

There were lines of boot tracks leading away from all of the ships. Oliver, Stella and Amy followed the tracks, which led them to the mouth of a cave in a nearby hillside. They examined the mouth of the cave for a moment.

'This mouth of a cave ... ' said Stella.

'Yes?' said Amy.

'It's a bit odd-looking,' said Stella.

'I was thinking that,' said Amy.

'You see all those stalactites and stalagmites in there?' said Stella.

'I don't think they're stalactites and stalagmites at all,' said Amy.

'Nor do I,' said Stella. 'I think they're—'

' ... teeth,' they said together. Then Stella added, 'This isn't the mouth of a *cave*, it's—'

‘ … just a mouth,’ said Amy. ‘What fun! And those pilots didn’t get eaten—’

‘ … so much as just walk into something’s mouth on purpose,’ said Stella. ‘I think that’s the oddest thing I’ve ever heard!’

Oliver was feeling a bit embarrassed for his fellow Space Mistakes. ‘In their defence,’ he said, ‘it might *not* be a mouth.’

‘Yes, but it is, though,’ said Stella.

‘I am not arguing with you, Stella,’ said Oliver. ‘We’ve come here to rescue the pilots of those crashed spaceships and that’s what we’re going to do.’

‘You’re not actually suggesting we go in there, are you?’ said Stella. ‘There won’t be anything of them left to rescue. They’ve been eaten.’

‘No, they haven’t,’ said Oliver.

‘Prove it,’ said Stella.

Oliver tiptoed over to the mouth of what he still hoped was just a cave. He put his head inside and called out, ‘Hello!’ Then he pulled his head back out again as quickly as he could.

‘Well, I didn’t hear anyone,’ said Stella.

Suddenly, a voice from deep down in the cave called out, ‘Hello!’

‘It’s an echo,’ said Stella.

‘Is there someone out there?’ the voice went on.

'Bother,' said Stella. 'It's not an echo.'

'That settles it,' said Oliver. 'We have to go in and rescue them.'

'No, we don't,' said Stella. She put her head in the mouth of the cave and called out, 'We've come to rescue you. Please come to the mouth of the cave at once.'

'No,' said the voice from inside the cave.

'Why not?' said Stella.

'We wouldn't *dream* of just coming out,' said the voice from inside the cave. 'You've come all this way to rescue us – you simply *must* come in for some tea first. We've got cake and everything.'

'Did you hear that?' said Oliver. 'They're still alive, so this is not a mouth after all, and they are offering us tea, so we have to go in.'

'Why?' said Stella.

'Because it would be rude not to, of course,' said Oliver, wondering quite where some people kept their manners.

'What if that's not them speaking?' said Stella. 'What if that is the voice of the monster whose mouth this obviously is? What if that's how it traps its prey, by mimicking the voices of things it's already eaten as a clever way of luring its next meal inside?'

'I say *cake*,' said the voice from inside the cave. 'I must warn you that it is a teeny weeny bit on the disgusting side, what with it being about ten years old now, but ... ' the voice brightened, trying its best to be cheerful, 'it could be worse. Not sure how, mind you!'

'What kind of monster is going to say something like that?' asked Oliver. 'Even as a trap?'

'Me first to get eaten!' said Amy, waving an arm in the air and jumping up and down.

'For the umpteenth time,' said Oliver, 'they haven't been eaten.'

'They might be being digested so slowly they don't even notice,' said Stella.

'All right,' said Amy. 'Me first to get slowly digested!' She bounded into what Oliver hoped against hope might still turn out to be a cave. 'Come on, you lot!' she called after them.

Stella and Oliver looked at one another and followed her inside.

If the cave was indeed a cave, it was doing a very good job of looking like the inside of a monster. Its walls were a sort of purply-pink insides-y kind of colour, and they were shiny with just the type of repulsive fluid you often found in monsters' mouths. As if that wasn't revolting enough, the floor of the cave was soft and undulating and, in certain lights, it looked an awful lot like a tongue.

Stella looked like she was about to say something when

Oliver spotted a light flickering at the back of the cave.

'That's them,' said Oliver. 'Not far now.'

There were twelve Space Mistakes in all, huddled around a small campfire. They were all different shapes, sizes, species and colours. They were thin and miserable-looking, though struggling nobly to put a brave face on things, and their uniforms were ragged and dirty from years of wear.

There was something else they all had in common.

'They're all just like you,' Stella and Amy whispered to Oliver simultaneously.

'Nonsense,' said Oliver, but he knew they were right.

Their friendly smiles and their cheerfulness despite the dreadful circumstances – even their insistence on having tea while sitting in what might be the belly of a monster – was all exactly the way he would have behaved.

'Did you come far?' asked one.

'Lovely weather we've been having,' said another.

'Do please sit down and have some tea,' said a third.

'Though it isn't really *tea* as such,' said a fourth.

'No,' said a fifth. 'We ran out of real tea some years ago. This is sort of—'

'I think the less you know about how we make it,' said a sixth, 'the more you'll enjoy it.'

'Thank you,' said Oliver, who was the only member of

the crew who took a cup. 'It is an interesting taste, isn't it?' he said, after trying the tea and just about managing not to be sick.

'Though of course I'd really love a cheese and pickle sandwich,' said a seventh Space Mistake.

'So how did you all end up here?' asked Amy.

'Let me guess,' said Stella. 'Your computers warned you to change course but you were so completely lost in the beauty of space that you forgot.'

'Spot on!' said the Space Mistakes all together.

Oliver looked around at the Space Mistakes and a terrible thought filled his mind. If it hadn't been for Amy, Stella and Brumph being around to save him every time, he too would have ended up stuck in some miserable cave for years on end.

'All right, Captain,' said Stella. 'Who are these people, and why are they so much like you?'

Oliver knew there was no point keeping the secret any longer. 'Oh, all right, they're Space Mistakes, OK?' he said. 'Useless men and women who can't do anything right so they've been sent out here to the farthest corner of the universe where they'll do less damage.'

'Steady on, old boy,' said the first Space Mistake. 'That's a jolly hurtful thing to say, you know.'

'How do you know, chief?' asked Amy.

'Because I'm one too,' said Oliver. 'I'm sorry, I should have told you years ago when we started this mission. Why do you think I keep getting everything wrong?'

'But you don't,' said Stella. 'Not *everything*.' Before Oliver could reply, Stella's wrist communicator started flashing and she answered it. A funny-flavoured smell came out of it.

'Brumph says there's an emergency back on the ship,' Stella translated. 'We have to get back there immediately.'

'Emergency?' asked Amy. 'What kind of emergency?'

The sounds of a struggle – and the smell of potting compost – came from Stella's communicator, then a voice rang out: a voice the crew of the *Some Hope* recognized at once.

'Greetings, puny ones. Thanks to your carelessness,' said His Galactic Evilness, Gloth the dark lord of the Vespidrillion Empire, 'we have grown to an almighty size and seized your vessel, and the Eek-Drive that powers it. Soon it will carry us to the heart of the universe! Mwa ha ha ha ha!'

'How on earth could they have grown to an almighty size?' said Amy.

Stella thought for a moment, then she said, 'Where did you put Banjax's Enlarging Tube, Captain?'

'You didn't put it in the stationery cupboard next to the

flapjack box that had the Vespidrillion battleship in it, did you, chief?' asked Amy.

Oliver hung his head in shame and muttered, 'I told you. I'm a Space Mistake.'

Before Amy and Stella had a chance to say anything, something else rather unfortunate happened. Brumph's funny-flavoured smell message had floated some distance from Stella's wrist communicator. Tiny molecules of funny-flavoured smell had gone tumbling through the air until they had reached the walls of the cave and were absorbed by them.

Except that the cave wasn't a cave. It was – of course – the insides of a huge monster, though 'monster' is a bit harsh. It was the insides of a large space serpent called a Blim that had – just like the pilots – been so lost in the beauty of space that it hadn't noticed this little planet until it was too late, and had crashed into it.

Once on the planet, the Blim had decided to stay for a while, and had found a comfy-looking hillside and burrowed into it. Over the centuries, all sorts of creatures had used the Blim's insides as a shelter and a home. The Blim liked having company and did its best to keep its guests warm and safe.

The Blim was, however, allergic to funny-flavoured smells. The moment the first molecule of Brumph's funny-flavoured smell was absorbed by its stomach walls, the Blim started to feel very odd indeed. It shook, it roiled and it spasmed, causing everyone inside to be thrown about all over the place. The Blim gave a huge cry of discomfort.

'Well, that settles the "Is it a cave or is it a monster?" argument,' said Stella as she pulled herself up off a pile of recently collapsed Space Mistakes.

'Yippee!' said Amy. 'We've been eaten! Well, come on everybody, it's time to run!'

The Space Mistakes scrambled unsteadily to their feet and hobbled as fast as they could towards the mouth of the cave, which was now snapping open and closed.

'Oh, crumbling comets!' cried one.

Amy took control of the situation, picking up the pilots one by one and throwing them out of the Blim's mouth each time it opened. It was only once they were all safe that she noticed something. 'Where's the chief?'

'We must have left him back there,' said Stella. 'Maybe he got knocked out when we were all thrown around just now. I'll go and get him.'

She found Oliver sitting by the campfire. He hadn't been knocked out – he was just staring sadly into the flames.

'Come on, Captain,' she said. 'We have to go.'

'No, Stella,' said Oliver. 'You do. If I come with you, I'll only mess things up again, the way I always do.'

'You don't always mess things up,' said Stella.

'I've just made you walk into the stomach of a huge monster,' said Oliver.

'All right, there was that one time,' said Stella.

'I ruined any chance of peace with the party animals,' said Oliver.

'Very well then – twice,' said Stella.

'And just now, letting the Vespidrillions get hold of the Enlarging Tube,' said Oliver.

'Three times,' said Stella. 'But—'

'And I brought the universe to the brink of all-out war armed only with a blueberry muffin,' said Oliver.

'Tell me about it later,' said Stella, as the Blim's body started wobbling around them again. 'I'm not leaving without you,' and she held out one of her tentacles.

Oliver looked into Stella's eyes. He could see from the fierce determination in them that he wasn't going to be able to persuade her. 'You don't deserve to end up being wobbled to death inside the belly of a huge monster,' he said, 'and that's the only reason I'm coming with you.'

Amy was waiting for them at the mouth of the Blim. In daylight, the other Space Mistakes looked even more sick and frail.

'We have to get to the shuttle as quickly as we can,' said

Amy. 'If we don't get back to the *Some Hope* before those Vespidrillions blast their way to the heart of the universe, we'll be stuck here forever.'

'And there'll be no one to stop the Vespidrillions taking over the universe,' said Stella. 'Come on.'

'I'm sorry about this,' said the first Space Mistake, 'but our chaps aren't fast movers. Our legs are weak from hunger, disease and lack of use. You'd better go on without us.'

The Blim blinked its large, mossy eyes. The funny-flavoured smell had made it feel horrible, but that had gone now. Far more important to the Blim was seeing that its guests appeared to be leaving. That made the Blim unhappy because it had enjoyed their stay – so it decided to follow them and see if they'd like to change their minds.

Unfortunately, Stella, the only one of them who might have been expected to speak Space Serpent, had been ill the day that language was taught at the Academy. So when the Blim tried to explain what it was doing, all she – and the rest of them – saw was a huge monster bursting up out of a hillside, giving an ear-splitting roar and slithering towards them rather quickly while snapping its toothy jaws.

'Do you know what?' said the first Space Mistake. 'I do believe our chaps might just be able to move quite fast after all.' In fact, everyone surprised themselves with the speed at which they managed to reach the shuttle and scramble back inside.

Thinking about it a bit more, the Blim wondered if perhaps its guests were playing a game. They were running away because they wanted it to chase them. The Blim liked that thought and gave another happy roar before slithering even faster after them. Imagine its surprise when it saw its guests all trying to hide in a metal box! This really was a funny game. The Blim's guests obviously wanted the Blim to grab hold of their metal box and swallow it whole, so the Blim opened its huge jaws as wide as it could as the metal box rose up in the air.

The Blim was just about to close its jaws around the metal box when hot rockets blasted out of one end and caught the Blim right in the mouth! The Blim frowned. It was going to have a sore throat for ages now! As it watched the metal box fly off into the sky and disappear, the Blim hoped its next group of guests would be a bit more grateful.

***

Aboard the shuttle, Amy and Stella were already making plans for taking back control of the *Some Hope*.

'If you can bring the shuttle alongside the bridge,'

said Amy, 'I should be able to spacewalk across and get in through a service hatch. Then, while I'm tackling the Vespidrillions, the chief here can set Brumph free and—'

'No,' said Oliver. 'Don't trust me with anything important. I'll only make a mess of it.'

'Not again, Captain,' said Stella. 'We need you.'

'No, you don't,' said Oliver. 'This is all my fault. I will only make things worse.'

'Come on, old boy,' said the first Space Mistake. '*We'd* be helping them out if we weren't so dashed weak and frail. It's the decent thing to do.'

'And you'd mess it up too,' said Oliver. 'We're Space Mistakes, all of us, and that's what we do.'

'It's true that I did make a bit of a boo-boo back home,' said the first Space Mistake. 'But instead of exiling me, the Wise Brains sent me out on a very important mission.'

'Me too,' said another Space Mistake.

'And us,' said the rest.

'I alone was sent to bring peace to the farthest corner of the universe,' they all said together. Then they realized what they'd said and started looking round.

'No, you *weren't*, I was.'

'No, *you* weren't, *I* was.'

Oliver watched them argue for a moment, then he said, 'What interests me is that you've been stuck inside the belly of that monster for years and you've only just realized this.'

'We had a rule about not talking about work,' said the first Space Mistake. 'Oh, suffering solar systems.'

The shuttle's communication screen flashed into life. There was Gloth, the dark lord of the Vespidrillion Empire, now huge and horrible in his shining black uniform. Next to him was one of his henchmen, attempting to look scary even though he was wearing only his vest and pants. The henchman was clutching Brumph in one hand, and a bottle of weedkiller in the other.

'I see you are about to launch an attack, puny ones,' said Gloth coldly. 'I have your crew member at my mercy. If you do not surrender at once to my henchmen, I will be forced to have him – ' Gloth paused to think of something funny to say, '*weeded* out. Mwa ha ha ha ha ha.'

'What an absolute spoilsport,' said Amy. They couldn't risk anything bad happening to Brumph.

'We surrender,' said Stella.

***

They landed in the loading bay of the *Some Hope*. When the doors hissed open, the now full-sized Vlort and his full-sized henchmen were waiting, looking a bit chilly in their underwear but with their laser blasters at the ready.

‘Lock them up,’ said Vlort. ‘All but the captain, the first mate and the octopod. Handcuff them! They’re coming with me.’

The henchmen handcuffed Oliver and Amy quite easily but they ran out of handcuffs on Stella, and had to tie her last two tentacles together with ribbon from a birthday present.

‘The dark lord wishes to see you, Captain,’ said Vlort.

‘Is he going to crush me into space dust?’ asked Oliver.

‘He is going to thank you,’ chuckled Vlort wickedly. ‘Without your help, the entire Vespidrillion Empire would still be stuck in that beastly box in that wretched cupboard. Because of you, we’re about to take over the universe.’

Oliver hadn’t thought it was possible to feel any worse than he already did – but those words broke his spirit completely.

‘The dark lord will allow you to witness the triumph you made possible,’ said Vlort, ‘and *then* he will crush you – and your friends – into space dust. Wait here.’ He marched out.

‘Captain?’ said Amy.

‘It’s all right,’ said Oliver. ‘I don’t like people who say ‘I told you so’, so I’m not going to.’

‘It’s not that,’ said Amy. ‘I just wanted to know if … if I could call you Olly Jolly from now on.’

‘Of course you can,’ said Oliver. ‘I’ve always wanted you all to call me that.’

‘I thought it sounded a bit silly before,’ said Amy. ‘But I was wrong. I think it sounds kind and friendly.’

‘You’re a bit late for kind and friendly,’ said Oliver. ‘It’s scared and beaten time now.’

‘I disagree, Olly,’ said Amy. ‘I think this is just the time for kind and friendly.’

‘I’m sorry for not telling you I’m a Space Mistake earlier,’ said Oliver. ‘I thought if I did, you’d all laugh at me.’

‘*Me*, laugh at *you*?’ said Stella. ‘You do know that I only came on this mission to get away from people who laughed at me.’

‘Why would anyone laugh at you?’ asked Amy.

‘Because of my real last name,’ said Stella.

‘What is your real last name?’ asked Oliver.

‘Can you keep a secret?’ said Stella.

‘I don’t think we’re going to get a chance to tell anyone else,’ said Amy.

‘It’s *Argh!*’ said Stella.

‘Oh,’ said Amy.

‘No, *Argh!*’ said Stella.

‘I know that, I just meant … Oh, never mind,’ said Amy.

‘Why?’ said Oliver.

‘My parents love words,’ said Stella, ‘often without

knowing what they really mean.'

'Is that why you've learned so many languages?' said Oliver.

'I suppose so,' said Stella. 'It's also the reason why my parents changed our last name to their favourite word in the whole universe.'

'Which is *Argh*?' said Oliver.

'Actually, to pronounce it properly, you need to drop a toaster on your foot,' said Stella, 'but there isn't a toaster handy, so I'll overlook that.'

Oliver smiled. He was in a hopeless situation, facing almost certain death, but suddenly, because of his friends, things didn't seem so bad.

Then the doors swooshed open and Vlort returned.

'His Galactic Evilness will see you now,' he said.

***

Gloth was sitting in the captain's chair on the bridge. Oliver noticed that, even though he was now full size, his feet didn't quite touch the floor.

'The heart of the universe awaits us,' said Gloth. 'When I activate the Eek-Drive, we will ride to supreme power on a tide of war and destruction. The tears of the conquered will flow like rivers into a swamp of misery—'

'*Sea* of misery,' corrected Vlort.

'All right, all right,' said Gloth.

Amy and Stella had lifted Oliver's spirits. He felt his natural positivity stirring again.

'But you don't know the way,' he said, 'and you have to be just right with the Eek-Drive or you'll end up in a supernova or a black hole – burned to a frazzle or squished flat.'

'Your ship's computer has a GPS,' said Gloth. 'It's a Galactic Positioning System. We'll just ask it to take us Home.'

'Oh yes,' said Oliver. 'Of course.' He hadn't thought of that.

Gloth turned to a henchman sitting in the first mate's chair. 'Activate the Eek-Drive.'

The engines roared, the ship gave a lurch and the stars all around them turned to streaks as the *Some Hope* tore through space at a fantastic speed.

'Hang on, though,' said Oliver. 'This is a peace mission. Our ship has no weapons. Even if you do reach the heart of the universe, you won't be able to do any damage.'

Gloth snapped his fingers and pointed out of the window. Oliver looked out to see that the Vespidrillion battleship's cannons had been bolted on to the sides of the ship.

'We have quite enough fire power to bring your

civilization to its knees,' said Gloth. He pointed to a special control console the Vespidrillions had rigged up next to the hot chocolate machine. In the middle of it was a big red button with 'Fire' written on it so he wouldn't forget what it was for.

'All I have to do is press that button,' he said, 'and everyone you have ever known or cared about will be space dust. Eek!'

'Are you all right, Your Galactic Evilness?' asked Vlort.

'I'm fine,' said Gloth, who actually looked very shaken up. 'I'm just not used to arriving somewhere so quickly.' He straightened his uniform and said, 'And now ... *it begins*.'

Oliver looked out of the window. The *Some Hope* had come to rest out of Eek-Drive right in front of the Palace of Universal Peace.

'Now that's a pretty building,' said Vlort. 'Why can't *we* have buildings like that? It's made almost entirely of golden glass – it must be like walking into a starbeam.'

'Stop babbling – it's time to attack!' snapped Gloth.

Gloth pressed the communication button on the arm of the captain's chair.

'Peoples of the Galactic Capital Planet,' his voice boomed out from the ship. 'Prepare to become prisoners of the dark lord and the Vespidrillion Empire.'

The main screen on the bridge flickered into life. The face of Oliver's dad appeared.

'Who is this?' he said. 'And what have you done with my son, the captain?'

'Your son is quite well,' said Gloth, 'for the moment, at least. It was he who made it possible for us to conquer your planet.'

'I don't believe that for a minute,' said Oliver's dad. 'My son has made mistakes, just like we all have, but I know that he has the capacity to be a hero. If he is in there with you, then he will be ready to foil your sinister plans.'

'Mwa ha ha ha ha,' laughed Gloth. He swung round in the captain's chair. 'What do you think, sonny boy?' he said to Oliver. 'Got any bright ideas?'

The henchman in the first mate's chair said, 'The weapons are primed and ready to fire at any moment, Your Galactic Evilness.'

'Surrender now,' said Gloth, 'or be crushed into space dust!'

'Never!' said Oliver's dad.

'Very well then,' said Gloth, and he turned the main screen off. 'Looks like time's run out to save your dear old dad.' Gloth hoisted himself out of the chair and walked towards the weapons control console.

‘I’ve got to do something,’ said Oliver under his breath. ‘You heard my dad – he’s depending on me.’

‘The weapons control console,’ whispered Stella. ‘It’s right next to the hot chocolate machine.’

‘It’s not really the time to think about getting yourself a drink,’ said Oliver.

‘What else did we put next to the hot chocolate machine?’ Stella hissed back.

‘The Surprise Machine!’ said Amy. ‘That’s brilliant! If only we could trip Gloth over before he gets to the console, he might accidentally press the button on the Surprise Machine instead of the one that’ll crush everyone into space dust.’

‘But if he does push it, what sort of surprise will he get?’ asked Stella.

‘I have no idea,’ said Amy, ‘but it’s the only chance we have. Except ... how can we trip him over?’

Gloth was more than halfway to the weapons control station before Oliver had a brilliant idea.

‘Cheese and pickle sandwiches!’ he said. ‘Stella, can you distract the guards?’

‘Of course,’ said Stella, and she flopped on to the floor, her tentacles flapping, and shrieked, ‘Oopsadaisy, I must have slipped.’

‘Silence!’ cried Gloth. ‘Guards, subdue that octopod!’

The henchmen grabbed Stella, but she managed to wriggle out of their grasp a few times before they finally held her fast. It was enough. Oliver just managed to get the sandwiches out of his pocket.

He felt them. They were still as 'refridgy-squidgy' as the day they were made.

There was no time to lose. Gloth was nearly there; in a few more seconds, he would be able to press the 'Fire' button. Oliver threw the sandwiches across the room. They landed – perfectly – just in front of Gloth.

His Galactic Evilness didn't notice them in time and brought his evil boot down evilly on them. His evil boot squidged and slipped. Gloth wobbled for a moment. He reached out to try to steady himself and just before flopping over and landing face down on the floor ...

... he pressed the button on the Surprise Machine.

Gloth and the other Vespidrillions didn't even have the chance to say, 'Well I never, now that *is* a surprise!' before they were once again shrunk down to their original size and trapped back in Oliver's flapjack box.

'Hooray!' cried Stella. She pressed the communication button on the arm of the captain's chair and announced to the terrified citizens outside the ship, 'It's all right, everyone! Olly Jolly's done it! He's saved the universe!'

***

What happened next felt a bit like a dream to Oliver. He and Amy, Stella and Brumph stepped out of the *Some Hope* to find the ship surrounded by cheering crowds. They were picked up and carried shoulder-high to the Palace of Universal Peace, where the Wise Brains floated out to greet them, the fluid in their globes bubbling with excitement.

'I knew all along he was going to save the universe,' said one Wise Brain.

'*I* did, you mean,' said another.

'I think you'll find,' said the Wisest of All Brains, 'that this was *my* brilliant idea.'

But Oliver didn't care, because his dad had come running out to hug him.

'You're safe!' said his dad joyfully. 'And what's more, you're a hero!'

There was more cheering, a lot of it, and that was not – as Oliver found out during the weeks that followed – *always* the best thing to happen to you. The vast majority of the countless different peoples of the countless different planets cheered by making some kind of loud, excited noise, and that was fine. Some, though, cheered by blowing raspberries right in your face, or by shrieking 'Fleppum! Fleppum!' in your ear until you fell over, or by pouring jam down your trousers.

Oliver knew they meant well, but still: it wasn't much fun coming home after a long day of being celebrated to find that you had eyebrows full of spit, throbbing eardrums and blackberry-and-apple-flavoured pants.

So the day Oliver and the crew of the *Some Hope* were awarded their medals for saving the universe was also the day Oliver made a very important decision.

He and the crew, all wearing their smartest uniforms, lined up in front of an audience made up of all the most important people in the universe. Behind them was a display of items from their travels: the Surprise Machine, the squidged-up refridgy-fresh packet of cheese and pickle sandwiches and the transparent flapjack box that contained the most dangerous villains in the whole universe.

His Coolness, King Serenity the Untroubled, probably the wisest – and, after a long lie-down in a darkened room, once again the most relaxed – being in the universe, handed them their medals and even gave Oliver a blueberry muffin to show there were no hard feelings.

To huge applause, Oliver's dad announced that Oliver, Amy, Stella and Brumph had all been offered wonderful jobs at the Ministry of Universal Harmony.

When the applause finally died down, Oliver replied, 'Thank you, Dad, but I've decided: no thank you. You see, it turns out I rather like being out there, in the farthest corner of the universe – making friends, discovering new planets and having adventures.'

There was more applause, but King Serenity, for one, wasn't listening.

All this standing up had tired him out, and he was looking for somewhere comfy to sit down when he noticed the strange box, about the size of a suitcase, that was on stage behind him. Oliver caught sight of the King lowering himself wearily on to the single red button on the top of the Surprise Machine, and cried out, 'No, Your Coolness!'

But he was too late.

And what happened then?

Well, that *was* a surprise.

Where are they now?

Oliver Jolly

After a long career spreading peace throughout the universe (and only very occasionally bringing it to the brink of all-out war), he became a cake historian – or arcakeologist.

Amy Zone

Invented many more extreme sports, including Extreme Musical Chairs and Extreme Tiddly Winks (which were like the ordinary versions, only you did them in a volcano).

Stella Argh! (formerly Stella X)

Stella finally embraced her real last name and used it when she published a book of all the very rudest words in the universe. Her parents were extremely proud.

Brumph

Fired from Skyfleet for creating a stink in an enclosed escape pod. Went on to write the bestselling book, *Begonia with the Wind*.

Oliver's dad, Alastair Jolly

Served as Minister for Universal Harmony for many years after his son famously (and surprisingly) saved the universe. His brand of cheese and pickle sandwiches *(The Elevenses of Champions!)* became hugely popular.

King Serenity the Untroubled

Had a brilliant idea for something really interesting, fun, tasty, exciting, a little bit dangerous and totally brilliant. But couldn't be bothered to get out of bed to do anything about it and has now forgotten exactly what it was.

About the author

I began my adventures in space and time at a very young age when – much to my surprise – I was born. Ever since, I've tried to make sense of things by telling stories about them. I've written over 60 books (which took me *ages*) and they've been translated into 22 languages (which took someone else ages). My first books had huge long titles, such as *Mungo and the Picture Book Pirates* or *Guess What I Found in Dragon Wood*, but I've calmed down a bit since then and now my books are called things like *Soon, Extinct, What Next?*, *Dinosaurs in the Supermarket* and *Superhero Mum.*

Science fiction and comedy have always been two of my favourite things, so I hope that *Space Mistakes* – a science fiction comedy – is at least twice as good as most normal books. See what you think!